Fuchsias

HERMAN J. DE GRAAFF

REBO
PRODUCTIONS

© 1997 Rebo Productions b.v., the Netherlands
© 1997 Published by Rebo Productions Ltd.
jacket design: Ton Wienbelt, The Hague, the Netherlands
photography: Nico Vermeulen
editor: Elke Doelman
TextCase Boekproducties, the Netherlands
Typesetting: Hof&Land Typografie, the Netherlands
translation: Euro Business Translations, the Netherlands

ISBN 1 9010 94 73 1

Table of contents

Preface

Do you know many shrubs which bloom continuously from the middle of May until the first night frost? The fuchsia is one of these and that, of course, contributes to its enormous popularity. In addition there is the immense variation in colour, form and manner of growth. But all that glitters is not gold. For almost half the year, most fuchsias are not in the garden, but elsewhere, preferably in a moderately heated greenhouse. And then, what the greatest drawback for me is; they do not have the delicious fragrance which befits their elegance. But you can't have everything.

All in all, the genus Fuchsia offers us a group of striking, decorative plants which can be used almost anywhere in the garden, without being unusually demanding. For anyone who wants to use them exclusively as perennial border plants there is still a choice from about fifty hardy species and cultivars. And those who prefer to use them as annual bedding plants for only one season get real value for their money. There is hardly a plant to be found about which so many books have been written as the fuchsia, especially in recent years.

In the Netherlands, of course, we had some catching up to do, because after Witte's book (1882) no one had ventured to write about fuchsias. In the meantime we now have a list of about a dozen books, not counting those which have been translated for use in the Netherlands. In practice we can differentiate between three types of books. Firstly there are the books in which the emphasis lies on all sorts of things which are concerned with the culture of fuchsias.

The second category comprises books which give lists of as many species and cultivars as possible, with descriptions and preferably pictures of the plants and flowers. Thirdly there are books in which both aspects are discussed in combination. This book belongs, as do the majority in fact, to the last cate-gory, and the fuchsia culture receives most of the attention, certainly in the text. The photography will provide the enthusiasts with plenty of compensation.

This book takes you on a never-ending journey through the year, from spring, when everything starts to grow, up to and including winter – always a difficult time for our fuchsias – after which, year after year, that miracle happens: as soon as the days begin to lengthen, little green tips appear again on all those barren fuchsia branches and the whole cycle begins again.

H.J. de Graaff

Fuchsia fulgens 'Gosselli' can be recognised by its large heart-shaped leaves which are pinkish-red to dark green in colour.

CHAPTER I

The history of the fuchsia

This first chapter briefly sketches the history of the fuchsia, from the oldest fuchsias, to their introduction into Europe and the first hybrids which soon followed.

'Sipke Arjen' is an encliandra cross, named after Dr. S.A. Appel, a famous man in the world of fuchsias.

Right: 'Alabama Improved' is an old cultivar from the legendary English grower, James Lye (1871).

Very long ago, at least 50,000,000 years, the first fuchsias probably grew in the southern part of South America. At that time a favourable climate for fuchsias prevailed there – not too hot, but not too cold either.

Giant reptiles, the saurians, had been extinct for some time and had made room for all kinds of groups of mammals and birds. It was these birds which played an important role in the life of the fuchsias. Carboniferous forests with giant horsetails (*Equisetum*), primeval ferns, metres high, sigillaria trees and any other vegetable matter which can be found in our ordinary coal, had given way to forests of the type we now know.

Descendants of these immense, primitive plants now only play a modest role as undergrowth. At

Fuchsia cinerea is one of the most striking species, which is not too difficult to grow. It is easy to overwater and therefore needs a light soil. Be careful not to overfeed.

'San Leandro' is suitable as a shrub in the sun.

'Wilson's Joy' provides very floriferous shrubs.

that time there were still no humans of course, but the first primitive apes were already present. With the first fuchsia, a star was born which was to radiate over the non-frozen part of the Antarctic to New Zealand and Australia and

'Ringwood Market' is a floriferous and undemanding fuchsia.

Fuchsia regia reitzii is not hardy.

Fuchsia hartwegii is easy to grow and is a very beautiful fuchsia with clusters of blooms.

along the cool mountainous west ridge of the South-American continent into Mexico.
And very much later, with the help of humans, even as far as Europe and every part of the world where plant-lovers found a suitable climate for

'Mina Knudde'. This Belgian cultivar needs a spot in light shadow.

cultivating fuchsias. Finds of fossilised pollen provide undeniable proof that fuchsias grew in Australia about 30,000,000 years ago, although only for a short time.

In New Zealand they were able to hold their own and we still find three species there which strongly deviate from the American fuchsias. These include the creeping *F. procumbens* with striking blue pollen and a mainly yellow flower. In Mexico, the furthest spread area of the genus on the continent of America, species of fuchsia also grow which strongly deviate. They have very many small flowers, often in the branched clusters of the lilac-like fuchsias (section *Schufia*), such as *F. arborescens*.
Unlike most of the other species of fuchsia, they are not pollinated by birds feeding on the nectar,

Fuchsia andrei doesn't like the cold and needs light ground as a container plant in semi-shade. Overwinter in the greenhouse.

Fuchsia sessilifolia *The leaves are more striking than the somewhat pale flower clusters. Keep in green leaf in the greenhouse during the winter.*

Left: 'Waternymph' is a real fuchsia for enthusiastic beginners.

Below: 'Waternymph' was introduced as early as 1859. So it is a very strong cultivar.

Fuchsia hatschbachii *is a species related to* F. magellanica. *It grows rather more wildly and in the area where it originated can 'climb' 5 m into trees. It is possibly hardy.*

but simply by insects. In the region where it all started for the fuchsia, the species of the section *Quelusia* are found, to which *F. magellanica* belongs, the species that must be seen as the most important ancestor of almost all cultivated fuchsia cultivars.

Fuchsia procumbens *is a real "outsider" and comes from beaches in New Zealand. The plant is easy to get along with. The grape-sized berries have a real decorative value. It is a creeper.*

Fuchsia arborescens *is a splendid species for enthusiasts with a large garden. It flowers very early in the greenhouse.*

Changes through adaptation

On the long journey from the southern tip of America to inside Mexico, the descendants of the primitive fuchsia underwent many changes. In order to survive they had to adapt continually to their new surroundings. Thus, in a desert-like area along the coast of Chile we find overgrowth which strongly reminds us of the southern French maquis, *F. lycioides* (section *Kierschlegeria*) with thorn-like branches. In a dry area such as this, where succulent green is a rarity, this prickly character forms an excellent means of discouraging grazing by larger herbivores.

Left: 'Agnese Schwab'.Unfortunately, the photo does not show the aubergine colour of this novelty. Beautiful, but watch out that you don't give it too much water.

Below: 'City of Pacifica' is a semi-trailer with large, decorative blooms..

More towards the north, therefore closer to the equator, where dry, hot periods make life very

Fuchsia magellanica *Elegans' is one of the many hardy magellanica forms. It is possibly identical to* F. magellanica longipendunculata.

Below: Fuchsia sanctae rosae *is a very beautiful species.*

Fuchsia fulgens *'Jalisco' is one of the many forms of* F. fulgens, *which originates from Mexico.*

difficult for fuchsias, species occur with large tuberous roots, such as *F. inflata* (*Hemsleyella* section).

Thanks to these tuberous roots, like those of our potato and the dahlia, these plants are able to more or less miss an unfavourable part of the year. In the tropical region of northern South America though, in the cool and very wet mountainous forests, the most important group of fuchsias, from a botanical point of view, developed. This was the section *Fuchsia*, comprising over 60 different species. By their mostly long flowers with relatively small sepals and petals, they do not much resemble fuchsias of the *magellanica* type.

Since, like all green plants, fuchsias need a lot of light for their growth, they are found especially

Fuchsia boliviana *ssp.* boliviana *is a splendid species with enormous clusters of fruit. This species requires sun and space and is an excellent container plant.*

Fuchsia fulgens rubra *'Grandiflora' is a form of* F. fulgens *which needs a lot of space. It is a container plant requiring a sunny position.*

'Alberttina' will form a good-sized shrub in a light position. The plant was introduced in 1988 by the Dutch hybridist Netjes.

in open spaces in the forest or in places with low vegetation.

And yet, there are species which, with liana-like branches meters long, more or less climb into the surrounding spinneys. There are even species which grow on trees as epiphyte. In all, we are talking about a group of plants which combines a large area of spread with an enormous wealth of forms.

Fuchsias in culture

F. boliviana from the section *Fuchsia* was regularly found far from the spread area of the species found in the wild. Originally this was a mystery for horticulturists. Nowadays we know, however, that this plant with large clusters of

'Machu Picchu' flowers in Australia throughout the year. It is one of the best De Graaff introductions. It is problem-free in cultivation.

'WALZ Parasol' is a semi-trailer for a light spot.

edible berries was certainly grown by the Indian population of America for its fruits, but possibly also for the beautiful flowers. *F. boliviana* is especially found in the neighbourhood of old Indian settlements as a kind of traditional covering for old farmhouses, burial grounds, etc. I myself have had a *F. boliviana* for years, obtained from seed which was gathered in the old Inca temple city, Machu Picchu. I also named a rather wild-looking cultivar after this monument to a devastated civilisation.

Introduction into Europe

In the 17th and 18th centuries, sea-faring countries sent their trading fleets out all over the world. It was not unusual to send plant-collectors along on these expeditions. As a result of this, many exotic plants, naturally in the first place edible plants, spices and medicinal herbs, found their way into Europe.

The first potatoes, tomatoes, but also tobacco came to us in this way.

This overseas trade brought great wealth and thus a privileged class came into being with large country houses, which in Holland for example, can still be seen along the river Vecht and in the dunes area, where merchants from Amsterdam and their families went to relax. In their gardens, often with heated greenhouses, there was room for new exotic plants.

This made it attractive for the plant-hunters to bring back plants exclusively for their decorative value. The French monk/plant-hunter Charles Plumier (1646-1706), who while in the service of Louis XIV, the Sun King, went on these over-seas expeditions, had the honour of having introduced the fuchsia into Europe. It almost certainly did not involve living material but there was enough to describe the new plant well.

Fuchsia magellanica 'Variegata' is a striking hardy fuchsia.

Left: 'Leonhart von Fuchs'. A difficult variety to grow, but with magnificent flowers.

Below: 'Glenby' doesn't like a lot of sun. This bushy cultivar can bloom profusely.

Below: 'Gartenmeister Bonstedt' from 1905 is one of the first triphylla hybrids.

He named the first fuchsia in his description in *Nova Plantarum Americanarum Genera*, Paris 1703, after the German botanist he admired, Leonard Fuchs (1501-1566) *Fuchsia triphylla flore coccineo*, the three-leaved fuchsia with red flowers. Today, scientific plant-names consist only of the generic name followed by the name of the species, in accordance with the classification established by Linnaeus. The plant is therefore now called *Fuchsia triphylla*. For a long time we thought that it was not until 1788 that the first fuchsias were successfully grown in

Right: 'Delta's Delight' requires semi-shade. The small outstanding flowers on a self-branching bush do honour to the name of this cultivar.

'Elfriede Ott'. Nutzinger, grower of this cultivar, had, at an early stage, already seen the value of making use of species for hybridising. Here it is a matter of a cross between F. triphylla 'Koralle' with F. splendens.

Europe. It concerned species from the *Quelusia-*section, namely *F. magellanica* and *F. coccinea*. Since both species look very alike, there is some confusion regarding the names. It is, therefore, difficult to say which of the two was imported first. In the meantime it is highly likely that a fuchsia was already being cultivated in England 60 years earlier, albeit for a short time only.

In Philip Miller's *Dictionary of Gardening* 1739, there is a description of his experiences with *F. triphylla*, grown from seed collected by Dr William Houston on one of the French islands of America. Miller was head gardener of the 'Chelsea Physic Garden' from 1711 to 1770 and reports extensively on his cultivation experiences. From his account it appears that he must have had thorough knowledge of the cultivation of this notoriously difficult fuchsia

species. It is certain that until just before he died, Houston collected seed on the West-Indian islands such as Hispaniola. That Miller was the first European to grow fuchsias is the obvious conclusion. Every expert knows that *F. triphylla* is one of the most difficult species to grow, especially in the winter. It is therefore not surprising that Miller's success was short-lived and had no influence on fuchsia cultivation in Europe. It wasn't until around 1900 that growers, mostly German, came onto the market with crossings of *F. triphylla*, the well-known *triphylla* hybrids. 'Gartenmeister Bonstedt', Bonstedt 1905, is still a popular example of this.

The great breakthrough

Only at the end of the 18th century was there a real breakthrough for the fuchsia in Europe.

'Trailing King' is just like the 'Queen' a real trailer with somewhat softer-coloured blooms.

'Daniela', a well-branching dwarf. requires a spot with diffused light.

The first fuchsia described in *Icones Plantarum Rariorum*, Haarlem 1793, originally received a different genus name: *Nahusia*. This was in honour of the botanist professor A.P. Nahuys. The professor did not have much pleasure from the name for long, however. *Nahusia coccinea* is now again rightly called *Fuchsia coccinea*: not only is there, in spite of clear differences in outward appearance, great similarity to the *F. triphylla* described earlier, but both species can also be crossed successfully and, in a few cases, the products of the crossings are fertile.

Left: 'Veenlust'. A recent acquisition from Mr. Jansink (1995). This cultivar is best grown as a trailer.

Right: Fuchsia magellanica 'Variegata' is a variegated foliage mutant sport of F. magellanica with the same characteristics.

Below: When the calyx of the ripe flower is horizontal, the 'Queen of Derby' is a picture. It is an upright bush which requires diffused light.

'Rina Felix' is, as far as colour is concerned, a striking fuchsia, with New Zealand blood. Good feeding is needed.

Right: Fuchsia fulgens ssp fulgens is an easy species to grow. It has beautiful clusters of berries.

Following page: Fuchsia venusta is a beauty which never blooms if pruned back too hard.

The rule is that the earliest description applies, and the genus Nahusia did not materialise. Living plants of *F. coccinea* had been brought back though, and together with the probably simultaneously imported *F. magellanica*, which was added to the Kew Gardens collection in London in 1778, these formed the foundation for our fuchsia hobby.

A charming story about bringing the *F. coccinea* onto the market was told in 1882 in *Floralia*, a small handbook on the knowledge and cultivation of fuchsias. This, the oldest work in Dutch about fuchsias, was written by H. Witte, chief horticulturist of the hortus botanicus of the University of Leiden:

"Towards the end of the last century old Mr Lee was one of the most prominent horticulturists in the London area, so much so that several plants bear his name. Once, when one of his friends visited him, and they were walking through the greenhouses together, when the friend remarked: -You have many beautiful flowers, but if you had been with me in Wapping this morning you would have gazed on a flower which, in beauty and grace, surpasses everything I have seen here. –What did you say? And at which florist's was that? –It was not at a florist's, but at a simple captain's widow's house. –Hm! I'm sure it was beautiful. And what did this miracle look like; what was it? – I don't know what it was. I've never seen a plant like it before. Imagine a small shrub with beautiful pendulous crimson flowers, dark purple inside, and in such abundance that the branches looked indescribably beautiful, and so on. This was too much for Mr Lee. He asked for more information about the plant and the domicile of the widow, and, as soon as his friend had departed, hastened to Wapping where he soon found the widow's house. She really was in possession of a plant which, and the experienced horticulturist was in no doubt about it, was totally new in Europe: not only new, but so fantastically decorative, with such a profusion of blooms and apparently so easy to grow that it would be a gold mine for the first person who possessed it if he only knew how to exploit it. The old Mr Lee knew how to do this, as was soon to appear."

After some bargaining, Lee and the widow agreed that, for eight guineas he could take the

'Mary' is, on account of its foliage, a striking triphylla hybrid from the earliest days of this group.

'Traudchen Bonstedt'. Triphylla *hybrid from 1905, named by* Gartenmeister Bonstedt *after his daughter. Can tolerate full sun.*

'Corallina' var. tricolorii *is the variegated sport of 'Corallina'.*

Following pages: The national fuchsia exhibition in Zeist (the Netherlands), 1995

plant back to his place of work. He promised her that, in view of its sentimental value (the widow had received the plant from her late husband) the first young plant would be brought back to her.

The next spring, as the story goes, Lee sold 300 plants at a guinea a piece and so made a good profit in a short time.

The earliest crossings

Even before there was any question of Mendel's laws, people were industriously crossing with the materials at hand. For the formation of the greater part of the current cultivar stock we must assume the use of *F. magellanica, F. coccinea, F. fulgens, F. splendens* and *F. boliviana*. In the second edition of his book *Histoire et Culture*

du Fuchsia dated 1884, Felix Porcher already reports 520 different cultivars and also writes about the import of a whole series of fuchsia species in the first half of the 19th century: *F. lycioides* in 1796; *F. excorticata* from New Zealand, where it grows into a tree more than 10 metres high, in 1821; *F. arborescens* in 1823; *F. macrostemma* in 1825; *F. microphylla* in 1827; *F. fulgens* in 1837; *F. corimbiflora*, but more likely *F. boliviana* in 1839; *F. splendens* in 1842 and *F. venusta* in 1850.

Not until the end of the 19th century did the German growers get started with the (difficult to maintain) species, *F. triphylla*, as a successful

parent of the *triphylla* hybrids. 'Mary' and 'Traudchen Bonstedt' are the results of crossings dating from that period. Only in the last 25 years of this century has the larger part of the more than a hundred existing species been used, in particular by Dutch hybridists. It must be said here that the pioneer's work was carried out by the Austrian Karl Nutzinger and in even greater measure by the British researcher-hybridist John Wright.

Mutations

Sometimes, but rarely, plants and animals are found in the wild which deviate from normal. For example, for years a Spanish zoo has had a white gorilla, captured in Africa. And likewise I

once found a normal shrub heather with white flowers during a military exercise on the

'Berba's Trio' - without grafting it produces plants with different coloured flowers. Plants cultivated from cuttings with red and white flowers have lost this property.

'Tom West'. An old variegated foliage variety, which is possibly hardy if in a sheltered spot.

Below: Fuchsia fulgens 'Variegata' is the variegated foliage form of F. fulgens, which was discovered recently.

'Thalia' is a much-cultivated triphylla hybrid. Needs a lot of sun.

'Rika' is one of the earliest Dutch introductions by Hans van der Post. It must be topped in spring.

moors. Wild species which look normal can also possess such changed hereditary properties which, however, are not visible because they are dominated by the genes of the normal 'wild type'. As a result of self-pollination by such plants these properties can, however, be manifested. Drude Reiman, for example, who was the first person in Holland to possess a large collection of wild fuchsias, grew the white *F. triphylla* 'Challenge', obtained from the seed of *F. triphylla* by spontaneous self-pollination. Unfortunately, this difficult to cultivate form has been lost.

The British grower Edwin Goulding obtained the white *F. triphylla* 'Our Ted' through the self-pollination of *F. triphylla* 'Thalia'. Mutations or sports also occur regularly in natural circumstances. The results of these are usually less able to sustain themselves and the result is that they disappear again. Only if a wild mutant possesses

properties which are superior or at least as good as those of the normal organisms, is there a future for the deviating form. The white gorilla would almost surely not have survived in the wild, if only due to the lack of protective pigmentation against the rays of the sun.

People have an almost morbid preference for abnormalities. You can see that in gardens and parks. We love black pansies, although the flowers are practically invisible to their pollinators. We plant, for example, special species of beech trees such as red-leaved or weeping shapes instead of the natural green forms.

Actually this applies for most cultivated plants. That in 1840 the first fuchsia cultivar 'Venus Victrix', with a white tube and sepals; in 1848 'Mrs Storey' with white petals; in 1850 the first double 'Duplex' and 'Simplex' came onto the market and in 1853 the first variegated *F. variegata* was introduced and we have since recently had a variegated form of *F. fulgens*, are all results of the many crossings in which, completely coincidentally, invisible, mutated genes were combined.

The role of birds

In connection with pollination, fuchsias often have very long tube-like blooms. *F. gehrigeri* demonstrates this, although not in an extreme form. In my greenhouse, a *F. inflåta* had blooms with a length of 17 cm. Fuchsia blooms such as these are only pollinated by kolibris who, with their long bills and tongues, can suck nectar from deep inside the flower, where the nectar glands are situated. If a certain flower, by building in a chicane like this, can only be visited by one species of pollinator, the chance is greater that the pollen only reaches plants of the same species. This naturally increases the chance of pollination and seed formation considerably. Birds (fruit eaters) play yet another important

'Ratatouille' displays a rare colour combination. It is suitable either as a semi-trailer or as a broad shrub in partial shade. Introduced by Herman de Graaff.

Fuchsia gehrigeri cannot stand heat and prefers semi-shade. Do not give it too much water.

'Frozen Tears' is a splendid Dutch introduction from 1992 by Mario de Cooker. It is a trailer for semi-shade.

role in the life of the fuchsia: they eat the berries and so spread the seeds which are not digested over large distances – naturally dependent on the speed of the digestion process and the flight speed.

Late popularity in Holland

While in France and Britain in the last century, fuchsias galore could be admired in parks and gardens, interest in Holland was limited. In the U.K. the fuchsia, with all its elegance, was a symbol of the Victorian Age, while in Holland it remained a cottage garden plant, which, at the most, found a place on grandmother's cool windowsills. They were present though. When the gardens of 'Keukenhof' castle in Lisse got a face-

lift around 1860, as was the current fashion, the design for the garden made by the then famous landscape gardeners J.D. Zocher and L.F. Zocher, included many exotic plants. In a walled garden, round a Swiss-style summerhouse, you can still admire a broad hedge of what strongly resembles *F. magellanica* plants. They have been there since living memory and, in view of the history of the garden, that is at least since 1860, and have lost none of their beauty.

In late autumn they are cut down and covered with a thick layer of leaves and every summer there they are again, more than a metre tall and in full flowering glory.

Not until a hundred years later was the fuchsia really popular in Holland.

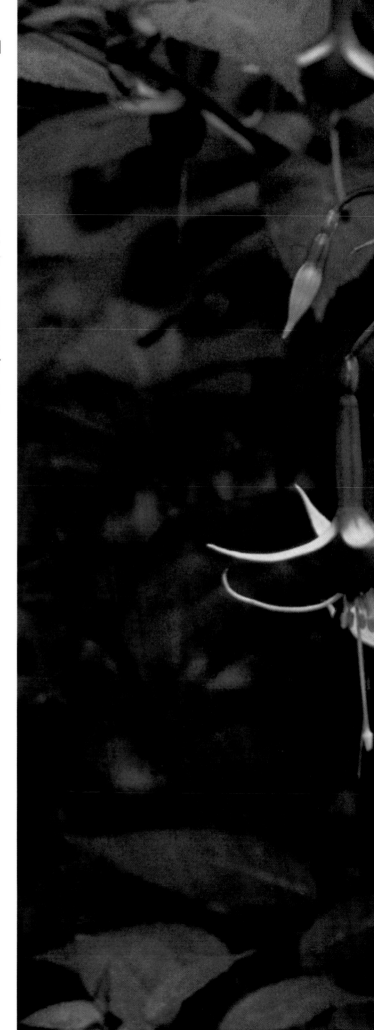

CHAPTER 2

Range, hybridising and exhibitions

Most fuchsias are upright growers, but some display trailing growth or are easy to persuade into this.

Both growth habits are discussed in this chapter, as is the hybridising of fuchsias in order to produce new shapes and colours. And where can the results of that hybridising work better be seen than at a national or regional fuchsia exhibition?

'Checkerboard' is beautiful, easy and no fuchsia collection would be complete without it.

Trailing fuchsias

Some fuchsias, such as 'Mantilla', 'Trailing Queen', the somewhat lighter coloured 'Trailing King' and 'Pink Rain' are born trailers. It is easy to make trailers from other cultivars if you can acquire the knack, even if the books say they are semi-trailers.

The very large-flowered cultivars, such as 'Taffeta Bow'. 'First Love' and 'Jubie-Lin' beg to be allowed to trail. They also like to trail in a sheltered spot because otherwise their rather delicate blooms can be quite severely damaged in the rather chilly, moderate climate which prevails here and in a large part of Northwestern Europe. Semi-trailers such as this and even upright cultivars can be transformed into trailers during their fast but weak growth in the greenhouse where there is a lot of heat and little light.

In Australia it is done by hanging small lead weights on the branches during the growing

'Doreen Redfern' is popular and not without reason. It does not tolerate sun.

In view of the shape of the corolla, 'Mantilla' is probably a descendant of a cross between F. triphylla *and* F. pringsheimii, *found in the wild.*

'Trailing Queen', one of the few real trailing fuchsias.

period. Once they have a good basic shape, the rest follows naturally. Trailers can be planted round the edges of hanging baskets. They can often mask the whole pot with their branches. Trailers of this kind are used to hang in pergolas

'Major Heaphy.' is a garden fuchsia that does not like dry conditions. The blooms display a combination of orange and purple.

'Trailing King' is one of the best trailing fuchsias.

or similar constructions. On a high tripod they can steal the show as a solitairy plant. The one-sided trailers fit against fences, sheds and house walls. Special pots with one flat side make hanging them up easier. This trailing shape is also perfect for positions in which the light clearly comes from one side. In containers on the balcony, trailing fuchsias can hide therailings under a curtain of green branches.

Upright fuchsias

Most fuchsias belong to this category. Upright fuchsias can grow into bushy shrubs which, depending on the species, can reach over 1.5 metres.

In sheltered gardens with little danger from gusts of wind, it is certainly worth cultivating deco-

'Taffeta Bow' is a large-flowered trailing fuchsia for a sheltered spot in semi-shade.

'Jubie-Lin' is a vigorously growing, large-flowered cultivar for a sheltered spot.

Left: 'First Love' is a semi-trailer with large blooms. It thrives in partial shade.

rative standards. To do this, allow a cutting to grow on without topping it, until it has reached the desired length, but pinch out the side-shoots. When the plant is tall enough, the side-shoots formed in the topmost 2-3 leaf axils can form the head. The stem must always be firmly tied to bamboo canes for support, because fuchsia wood is not very strong and can easily break in a gust of wind. Then all the trouble will have been in vain. See to it that the fasteners with which the cane is bound to the stem, do not get the chance to grow into the stem as this gradually gets thicker. If pots with tall plants do topple over in the wind, leave them lying down until the weather quietens.

Upright fuchsias can, of course, be dug in with pot and all to prevent toppling over. The wind will then no longer be a problem. You can also secure the pot by driving a piece of reinforcing steel bar into the ground and hooking it over the rim of the pot.

A beautiful fuchsia garden.

This garden is a sea of fuchsias.

Below: part of a fuchsia garden.

Above: 'Thamar' is an eye-catcher with blooms held outwards and upwards.

Left: 'Dennie Kaye' is an upright cultivar in shades of orange-red. This fuchsia tolerates sun.

Cultivating new forms

When the shadows begin to lengthen and the worst of the hot days have passed, and the humidity is a bit higher (in short, in the late summer), the hybridists take their chance. Although it is said that during that time the fuchsias make seed easily and that the end of their growing season is approaching, the prevailing humidity is probably the deciding factor. This should give the making of the pollen tube a better chance of success – the pollen tube guides the male cell nucleus from the pollen grain on the stigma to the female germ cells present in the ovary. After this has taken place, fertilisation can take place in the ovary and the development of the seed begins. True hybridists will try to cultivate new forms by artificial cross-pollination, whereby the attractive features of both parents are combined. Whether or not this succeeds depends purely on luck, but even luck can be helped along a bit. By cultivating large numbers of offspring from one particular cross, the chances of success are considerably improved.

Anyone interested in this can understand it by studying Mendel's laws. In order to produce a cross which is not influenced by undesired, coincidental pollination, only newly-opened flowers from the mother plant are used, in which no ripe pollen is yet present. The desired pollen is applied onto the stigma, the upper surface of the pistil. This is done with the aid of pointed tweezers, by brushing a filament with ripe pollen over the stigma.

After this, the stigma is covered, for example with a tube rolled from aluminium foil and

Greenpeace' was introduced by the author and has an exceptional colour combination. In the winter in the greenhouse the pale green with pale pink flowers grow in branched clusters.

pinched around the stamen. A label with the names of the parents is then fixed to the flower stem so that, if the embryo develops and makes seed, it will be known which crossing the seed originates from.

'Gregor Mendel' is beautiful but difficult. Beware of too much water and heat.

New forms and colours

The range of fuchsias we now know, and that comprises tens of thousands of cultivar names, has originated through the constant rearrangement of the genes in almost two centuries of cross-matching and the mutations which are manifested by this. Hybridising, certainly in fuchsias, from which about 20,000 names of cultivars are already known, only makes sense if the innovations produced are better than or different from the abundance of fuchsias already available. The addition of new introductions without reason, which look identical to a number of others, is rather annoying to those who want to have a correct name for their plants. Eventually it would be more difficult to recog-

nise the fuchsia cultivars than it already is. In the past 25 years Dutch hybridists have added many genuine new forms to the range by using wild parents for crossing which have not previously been used for hybridisation.

Left: 'Cor Spek' is a recent acquisition from Martin Beije. This upright cultivar has a preference for sun.

Below: 'Clair de Lune' is a French introduction from 1880 when orange was still rare in fuchsia.

'Hidcote Beauty' displays a beautifully coloured corolla. It is easy to grow.

'Wille Tamerus' is suitable for a window box in the sun.

This gave Dutch fuchsia hybridising an excellent name in the entire fuchsia world. The aubergine colour in fuchsias is largely thanks to the 'Dutch school', and the double orange was also added. Fuchsias with very long tubes, cultivars with flowers in branched inflorescence and small-flowered varieties are part of the contribution with which the Dutch have gained fame. A lot of investment has been made in recent years in the new fuchsia colour – yellow, al-though the chances are not very good for cultivating a fuchsia from seed with, for example, the colour of the related primrose. A start in the direction of this ideal is 'Space Shuttle' (de Graaff 1981), which in cool conditions has a yellow corolla, and 'Martin's Yellow Surprise' (Martin Beije

1994), with pale yellow sepals and petals. Fortunately for the crossers, there are enough other possibilities. The number of species, more than a hundred, present plenty of opportunities. Since only a small part of fuchsias which occur in the wild has been used, there is definitely still a future for fuchsia hybridising.

Previous pages: 'Heidi Ann' is a dwarf for semi-shade.

Below: 'Yolanda Franck' is one of the best Dutch introductions from Martha Franck. It is a strong plant which makes few demands and tolerates sun.

Above: the corolla of 'Zulu King' is almost black as it opens. In spite of the aubergine colour, this is a fuchsia you can do anything with.

'Fuji-San' is a striking introduction from the German Lutz Bögemann. It is an upright fuchsia.

'Zet's Alpha' is a striking introduction from the Dutch hybridist Zwier Stoel in 1993. It is easy to grow.

Looking at fuchsias

In the summer months, when the fuchsias are in full bloom and many gardens are a glorious sight, it would be a great shame not to share all this beauty with others. Therefore, many fuchsia-lovers are opening their gardens to the public. Fuchsia shows and exhibitions are also being organised throughout the country. As a visitor you can, of course, enjoy all the beautiful plants, But it is also handy get to know new varieties and pick up new ideas.

Seeing other fuchsia collections also provides the opportunity to find out the name of un-named fuchsias by comparing flowers, buds and leaves with other fuchsias. However, do not give a name to your nameless plant unless you are absolutely sure of it. Fuchsia growers in Holland

who are geared to selling to private individuals, often have open garden weeks, in which they display their mature plants in specially adapted

'Honnepon' has to be cherished in order to survive.

'Kwintet' is a strong cultivar with upright growth which was introduced by Van Wieringen in the early days of enthusiasm for fuchsias in Holland.

'Jack Shahan' is a plant for a cool place.

surroundings. One big advantage of this is that smaller versions of these plants are usually on sale, together with all kinds of things of interest to the fuchsia-lover.

National exhibitions

In 1965 the Dutch circle of friends of the fuchsia was set up, and with more than 5000 members is currently the world's largest fuchsia association.

Left: 'Willie Tamerus'. With the flower cluster at the end of the long branches.

Below: 'Phyllis is a good cultivar for enthusiastic beginners.

In a cool situation, 'Space Shuttle' displays a yellow corolla. The writer introduced this 'Speciosa'-descendant on the day that the first space shuttle was sent into orbit.

Left: Fuchsia 'Martin's Yellow Surprise'. Martin Beije with his 'surprise' -a fuchsia which in cool circumstances displays a lot of yellow. You mustn't give this one too much water.

It was the British fuchsia-lovers who inspired their counterparts in Holland and who originally imparted so much of their enthusiasm and knowledge to the Dutch. They now admire the new products of hybridisation and there has even been a very successful exhibition for which a collection of fuchsia trees from Lunteren, Holland, was sent across the channel.

Once every five years the national exhibition of the Dutch circle of friends of the fuchsia is held in a central location, usually in the park of a castle. At these exhibitions you can expect a broad overview of everything which is currently going on regarding fuchsias.

Naturally at an exhibition of this kind you can expect to find all kinds of things useful and otherwise, alongside books about fuchsias, and, of course, young plants.

Enthusiasts exchanging information during the national fuchsia exhibition in Holland.

Above: The national fuchsia exhibition in Zeist, Holland, 1995.

Below: During the national fuchsia exhibition in Zeist the fuchsias were displayed in natural surroundings.

'Party Frock' does justice to its name. It must be kept short to obtain a full, flowering plant.

For many this is an opportunity to meet other fuchsia-lovers from all over the country and naturally, to talk about fuchsias.
Information stands are there ready for your questions.

Regional shows

Usually a number of smaller-scale regional open-air shows are held in Holland during the summer months and these are spread throughout the country. Enthusiasts from regional clubs and circles supply the plants and do the work, sometimes aided by a professional arranger.

These shows attract many visitors who admire the breath-taking arrangements and the relaxed atmosphere. Indoor shows are disastrous for fuchsias if they last longer than a weekend.

'Alison Ewart' is at home everywhere and shows this with a profusion of small flowers.

Below: fuchsia garden 'Mercurius'/'Mrs Lovell Swisher'.

The plants begin to droop and soon lose their flowers and leaves in these conditions.

Open days

Many enthusiasts, but also nurserymen open their gardens or nurseries to the public for a few days during the summer. They make this known in local newspapers and club magazines and national gardening magazines.

Seeing the fuchsias in the garden where they have been grown brings a new dimension to the enthusiasm for fuchsias.

In the first place you can see what is really possible, and the owner can tell you how he achieved this. Problems which you have with your own fuchsias can sometimes be solved in this way.

Catalogues

Fuchsia growers bring out their new catalogues around January every year, in which they offer from several hundreds up to sometimes more than a thousand different species and cultivars. Often, the cultivars in the catalogue are listed according to their possibilities for use.

You will therefore find, in addition to the categories trailers and upright growing plants, *triphylla* hybrids (for sunny locations) and hardy fuchsias for perennial planting. The new acquisitions are usually a bit higher in price. As an enthusiastic beginner you should certainly limit yourself to the rather older cultivars, which have withstood the ravages of time.

Experimenting with novelties, which could still develop teething troubles, is more for those who are tired of the overwhelming existing range of fuchsias. When choosing new varieties don't only go by the information in the catalogue.

One of the many good books on fuchsias will often give a much more honest picture.

In general it is possible to visit the nursery of your choice in order to buy the young plants.

Most of the growers, even those abroad, are, however, prepared to send their products by post. They mention this in their catalogues, which can be sent to you on request, for a modest sum.

'Ketjil' is the Malay word for 'little one'. The small-flowered semi-trailer needs a cool position and care with watering. Introduced by the author in 1994.

'Goena-Goena'. (Black Magic). The dark corolla of the young flowers explains the name. The writer introduced this trailing fuchsia, which requires a cool place, in 1994.

CHAPTER 3

Fuchsias in all seasons

In this chapter, the annually recurring cycle of the fuchsia is discussed; from the joy of new life in the spring, to summer abundance, the melancholy and atmosphere of autumn and the bare stillness in winter, after which the cycle begins again.

'Eleanor Leytham' is a striking, compact dwarf with upward and outward pointing flowers and requires a sheltered spot in the garden without sun.

Spring

After a long, extremely cold winter there is still not much green, but the snowdrops and winter aconites are already producing pollen for the bees, which will be making the most of their chances as soon as the temperature rises to 9° C. In front of the beehives there is a flurry of activity from all the young worker bees getting their bearings. In spite of the long period of cold, all the bees appear to have survived. This also applies for the camellias which, dug into sphagnum peat, pot and all, and covered with a thick layer of dry leaves, have come through this experiment well. They are now covered in buds, which in the greenhouse would already have come out, but because it is so full they wouldn't have shown up well.

'Frank Unsworth' requires a light position. It is a self-branching semi-trailer.

'Merel' is an excellent trailer for a position in light shade. It is a beautiful introduction from the Dutch hybridist Mario de Cooker from 1993.

Some green can be seen in the evergreens, such as aucuba, box, ivy, holly and rhododendrons, and there are also some flowers, for example *Viburnum fragrans*, winter jasmine and the *Prunus autumnalis* which is again flowering, but for more we have to go into the greenhouse. If the winter has been less severe, there is more to be seen from the middle of March. Crocuses and early daffodils such as 'February Gold' and 'Tête à Tête' are already in full bloom until the first few warmer days, put an end to their flowering.

Spring-flowering bulbs are an ideal combination in a garden which houses a large collection of fuchsias in the summer. When the bulbs in the borders have finished blooming and are re-moved, the spaces which have been created can be filled with pots of fuchsias, dug in or free-standing. Where bulbs have been left to run wild, pots on tripod standards with a ring into which the pot fits can cheer things up a bit, without disturbing the plants which are dying off. The large-flowering tulip cultivars are unfortunately not suitable for running wild, but a number of wild species such as *Tulipa tarda* and *Tulipa urumiensis* can display their star-shaped flowers in large numbers in a sunny place in the garden, for many years.

They have the advantage that they are resistant to tulip blight. Daffodils run wild more easily, although the best results are obtained with the smaller flowered- varieties which are closer to the wilder form.

Unfortunately in my garden, which has rather a lot of shade, I have not managed to get jonquils such as 'Trevithian', double campernelles and the miniature 'Baby Moon' into bloom well the second year. I really appreciate their delicate fragrance and therefore replace them every year. There is, of course, a much wider range of spring-flowering bulbs and tubers: scillas, chionodoxas, erythroniums and, not forgetting, the many species of allium and frittillaria all give colour and flowers to the garden before the fuchsias make their entrance. The hyacinths, which spread their naturally delicious scent from the middle of April, form a rather stiff element for most gardens. They are better suited to park flower beds. With spring-flowering shrubs, all these together form a whole in which our fuchsias are not yet really needed. That soon changes: in summer the 'ballerina plants', which flower continuously until the end of the season with their enormous variation in growth and flowering, are an almost indispensable addition to every garden. However, before they are in place a lot has to be done, and that makes spring a very busy time for me.

A busy time

Spring seems to be the shortest season of the year for many of us. Not only have we just got over an apparently endless winter, but so much has to be accomplished in such a short time. It is alas a fact that many things need to be done at a

Fuchsia paniculata *is suitable as a solitairy tub plant and requires a place in the sun or semi-shade.*

certain time. If you haven't done some things in time, you will have to wait a whole year to reach the desired result. For fuchsias, for example, there is no point in taking cuttings after May 1st

'Wibke' is an attractive introduction from the well-known German hybridist Lutz Bögeman.

'Northway', with its upward and outward pointing flowers, is a striking sight..

if the intention is to enjoy beautiful flowering plants the same summer.

For many cultivars, topping after June 1st means that there can no longer be any chance of good flowering before the end of the summer. Spring is therefore rather a rush. Our plants are also in a hurry to get themselves ready for the rapidly approaching flowering season. We should be careful that, with all the potting, repotting, pruning, topping, taking cuttings, pricking out and possibly even grafting, we don't forget to enjoy all the new life this beautiful season brings. But about the middle of May, when all danger of night frost has passed, we must be ready to give our fuchsias a place in the garden. If we are too late with this, it is a pity for all the trouble we have taken, because the greenhouse is then too hot and too small for the rapidly growing plants. Owners of large gardens, with a reasonably sized greenhouse which can be kept frost-free, are privileged, especially in winter and spring. They don't first have to gather their fuchsias together from all kinds of storage places like the attic, the cellar or trenches. Everything is already in place and can develop according to the warmth and light available, until the moment that the plant can be exposed to the outside climate without too much risk. In a greenhouse, in early spring, you can also enjoy the winter- and spring-flowering fuchsias.

'Golden Treasure' is a variegated form from 1860 and excellent for low planting.

Summer

In Northwest Europe, where the climate is known to be very changeable, summer sometimes comes unexpectedly. While the last of the spring flowers, such as late tulips or the daffodil 'Baby Moon', are still in the border as a souvenir of an almost already forgotten period and the blackbirds in the garden can't seem to get enough food for their nestlings, summer suddenly arrives with a bang. Everywhere there is the fragrance of elder, mountain ash and hawthorn, and the colours of the rhododendron and laburnum are dominant. The carp in the streams have a great time now that the water is warm

Previous pages: 'Swingtime' has often stolen the show. It is probably identical to 'Stolze von Berlin' and needs a lot of light. It is an ideal plant for window boxes.

'Lark is a rather new triphilla *hybrid.*

'Mr A. Huggett' is an easy to grow, moderately tall shrub.

'Land van Beveren' is a striking acquisition from Flanders, which looks magnificent in a hanging container.

enough to spawn. In the pond their distant cousins, the goldfish, do their best to add to the overpopulation. The cats lie with half-closed eyes in a sunny spot. The heat hangs like a blanket above the green, which has now definitely burgeoned and displays the greatest imaginable variation in colour. It is, alas, also the time in which harmful insects begin to feel well and active and now is the best time to look out for possible damage. The best method of defence is attack!

Summer care

In summer a new regime applies for the care of fuchsias. Very shortly they will be dominating the garden with their unceasing flowering, and at twilight, when their colours become almost unreal, the honeysuckle joins the party with a matching perfume. It is time to give every tub plant, including the fuchsias, a fitting place in the garden. Most fuchsias are 'long day' plants, which means that they bloom in the summer. In favourable conditions they can keep this up until the first night frost.

For plants usually grown in a pot which is too small, they have to give a tremendous performance. They really only do this if the conditions are optimal - if after hardening-off we give them a good, light, but not too sunny place outside. Naturally, the ideal position is dependent on the species or cultivar.

For the more vulnerable, large-flowered plants you must look for a sheltered place. Furthermore, the whole arrangement must look attractive. Most fuchsia lovers find it difficult to accept that you can have too much of a good thing. To keep the plants in top condition you must give enough water, but not too much. Timely feeding must ensure that the plants do not fail partly through lack of food.

You won't hear me say that you have to talk to plants, but the idea of attention is of vital importance, particularly in the summer. You have to take a look at each plant every day, and as soon as there is anything wrong, take immediate action. Timely discovery of insects or the like, such as red mite, or a fungus, means you can fight the problem more easily. An invasion which is not spotted in time can necessitate the use of chemicals, which are never harmless.

In addition to this you must enjoy your plants because that's what it's all about. In the summer, every fuchsia-lover must enjoy the season through all his senses!

A wheelbarrow in the show garden of C. Spek, Heerde, Holland.

The right spot

Fuchsia blooms are at their best when their petals are visible. For the varieties cultivated as trailers that is not a problem: they come in hanging baskets, containers or hanging pots at or above eye level. For the upright habit growers, this is a reason to grow high shrubs or standards. Smaller bushy forms stand out best in raised borders, higher situated containers or large plant dishes. The few fuchsia forms with upward and outward pointing flowers, such as 'Minirose', 'Galadriel', 'WALZ Jubelteen' and 'Vobeglo', do very well as annuals in a low part of the border, in company with the eternal competitor, the pelargonium, and, for example., non-trailing lobelia species or heliotrope. Fuchsias with a large saucer-shaped corolla are well worth

looking at when seen from above. Try 'Loeky', 'Impudence' or 'Earre Barre' in a flower bed. For *triphylla* hybrids, with their clusters of tubular flowers, visibility of the small corolla is

'Koralle' has the characteristic inflorescence of the triphylla hybrids.

'Three Cheers', with its saucer-shaped corolla, is very suitable for bedding.

'Koralle' can grow to a full-sized bush in full sun in the garden.

'Galadriel' is hardy if you are lucky. To bloom profusely it must have a warm spot.

Fuchsia 'WALTZ Jubelteen' with box hedging in the garden.

Right: 'Earre Barre' stands out by the combination of aubergine and white. The corolla of this recent De Graaff-introduction is saucer-shaped when the flower is ripe.

of less importance. With their mostly orange-to-red flowers and bronzed foliage they are beautiful at any level. These are the only fuchsias which demand full sun. The others prefer various degrees of semi-shade, with as much light as possible.

Cultivars with light-coloured flowers, such as white, pink and all pastel shades, do not, on the whole, tolerate sun. The aubergine-coloured varieties such as 'Melanie' would be able to bear sun, but as descendants of species from the moderate New Zealand climate, with one or two exceptions, they do not like the sun's heat.

Fuchsias with orange flowers and combinations of a red calyx and a white, red or purplish blue 'skirt' are not so fussy.

As long as they are not in hot sun all day long, they can survive.

There are exceptions of course. The white 'Ting-a-Ling' makes a lot of buds in the sun, but to produce real white flowers it subsequently has to be put in the shade. So there is plenty of room for experiment, but you should assume that no fuchsia does well in deep shade.
They all need light for carbon-assimilation and growth.

Fuchsia 'Koralle' in the garden. Behind it is 'Kwintet'.

The last rose of summer
In many cases the last rose is a fuchsia flower. Fuchsias go on flowering until the first night frost, as long as they don't get too little light as a result of the sun getting lower and lower, and so they ensure a long summer in the garden. In temperate areas it is not unusual for fuchsias still to be in glorious bloom in the middle of October. In areas where a maritime climate prevails this doesn't always apply, due to factors like the strong south-westerly wind, which gets up sooner there and blows the flowers to pulp. The frequent gale-force winds are a sign that winter is on its way and the fuchsia season is coming to an end.

'Trumpeter' is a trailing triphylla hybrid, which threatens to be ousted by modern acquisitions.

Autumn

For some time now, the webs of the now fat diadem spider have been visible, fashioned into pearl necklaces by the morning dew. If possible I avoid them, because I am fond of my colle-ague-insect combatants, even though they are not very selective. The red admiral butterflies too, which have come after the windfall pears threaten to die in the spider's trap, just like the honey bees, which, although they have already been made ready for the winter with sugar, are still trying to collect as much pollen and nectar as possible for their last offspring. They have already killed the drones and this really brings the beekeeping season to a close. When the sun shines you can still enjoy so much beauty, al-though that enjoyment is tinged with a certain melancholy. It is the time of ripe fruits and leaves in autumn colours. In a garden where not all the dead branches and leaves have been

removed, toadstools and fungi now appear, which decompose the dead material into new plant material with their mycelium. In this way they are, together with the bacteria usually present in the ground, an important factor in natural recycling, and therefore they fit so well into the autumn, ushering in both the end and the beginning of the cycle. Where a leaf falls off, a new bud is awaiting the light and warmth of spring to awaken. And in the spring-flowering bulbs, the flower has already been formed. The natural process smells of autumn, which cannot be said of the compost heap, where the same process is taking place, only somewhat faster.

In the early evening, you can already vaguely pick up the scent of a couple of stray honey-suckle flowers, which again emphasise that

'Alison Ewart' with its outward pointing flowers lends itself well for flower beds.

Below: 'Celia Smedley' is a top fuchsia and can grow into an enormous tub plant in a short time.

summer has passed. It is time to get the non-hardy plants like the fuchsias ready for the winter.

Care

One day it's still summer and the plants are crying out for more water, the next day is almost wintry and the pot-compost remains wet. Watering has to be done carefully, only when necessary. Exactly the same applies for feeding. You can stop feeding normal cultivars during September. A number of more difficult varieties, such as descendants of *F. magdalenae*, only survive if they are wintered in the greenhouse. A small dose of nitrogen in the late autumn can be of help. Disinfestation is no longer really important, but red mite and fuchsia rust must be kept under control. Even in the autumn they can cause considerable damage. Combatting continues to be useful even if only to prevent infection of the garden and the greenhouse as much as possible. If rust starts in the greenhouse during the winter, in practice it is enough to fight it locally – possibly only by removing the affected leaves.

Preparation for the winter

Autumn is the season of melancholy. The last flowers of the summer disappear and, although the fuchsias hold out for a very long time, the decline is clearly setting in. Fortunately, there is another side to autumn. In this season we can enjoy the splendid colour of the leaves, with which nature adorns her farewell party. We harvest the fruits of the past season and, although few of us make use of the fuchsia fruits, we harvest the plants which have become big

Right: 'Autumnale'. The 'autumn coloured' leaves are unfortunately not visible on the photo.

Below: 'Celia Smedley' and 'Beacon' in the garden.

'Sunray' is a magnificent variegated cultivar which is at its best in the sun.

Left: 'Sleigh Bells' needs a sheltered spot.

Below: The still young flowers of 'Maori Maid' grow to sizeable flowers with a large, double corolla. It is a semi-trailer.

best branches will give a little more pleasure for a short time in a vase. Fortunately, the other side of all this demolition work is that it leads to a new beginning. Just like bare trees ready for the winter storms, those fuchsia plants reduced to ugly little stumps, hide the beauty of the new growing season. And yet, for me autumn remains a season of two faces: one face sad about everything that has been lost and one with the look of expectation for all the beauty waiting for us after the snow, freezing rain and cold.

The end of the season
The last leaves have fallen, the sky is grey and filled with the croaking of jackdaws and the screaming of gulls migrating inland.

'Florence Mary Abbott' is one of the most beautiful in the white genre, but needs a sheltered spot, out of the sun.

and strong in the summer. We must, of course, help them through the winter ahead and that brings a lot of work. Whatever we choose, a frost-free greenhouse, a trench, an old freezer filled with sphagnum peat or a place indoors in the attic, in the cellar, in the crawl space under the floor or just on the windowsill of a cool, but frost-free bedroom, the overwintering needs a lot of preparation.

Naturally there is nothing positive in having to cut back and pull beautiful flowering plants out of their pots. With a bit of skill and cunning the

The lapwings have long gone in search of the sunny south. Now that the fuchsias are gone and everything has been tidied up, the garden looks bare, although the autumn-flowering prunus and the *Viburnum fragrans* are doing their best. In the earth, the newly-planted bulbs are biding their time. Some more leaves over the hardy fuchsias and over the foot of the more or less hardy exotic plants such as camellias and, as far as I'm concerned: let the winter come!

Preferably starting with a thick layer of snow, because this gives the best insulation you could wish for and immediately dresses up the barrenness.

'Guurtje' is a semi-trailer, which does not easily tolerate heat. In cool conditions the sepals curve upwards and the flower shows up better.

Winter

In spite of all its serene beauty, winter is the great executioner, the season of cold death. Fortunately, this compulsory rest period is due to lack of light is not eternal rest for most plants and animals. Most of them survive, although for fuchsias this means a lot of effort on our part. For the annuals this really is the end. But the representatives of the native plants have of course long ensured the continued existence of the species through their usually abundant seed production, which after a period of cold will germinate safely in the spring. Many enemies of the fuchsia will, fortunately, not survive even though they have found a favourable spot for themselves or their eggs to prevent the worst.

'Mickey Goult' is an upright bush with outstanding flowers. It is an excellent bedding plant.

'Westergeest' is an unusual, problem-free upright fuchsia for a light location.

Hungry birds, such as the tits, in their diligent search for the scanty available food, succeed in finding many of these secret hiding places. Severe winters, which often mean the end of carefully built up fuchsia collections of owners who later became too nonchalant, ensure that there are no early attacks from aphids and other villains. The winter rest period offers us more advantages: with the help of new gardening books – perhaps Christmas presents? – we can make plans for which we have so far had no time. In newly-published catalogues we can already look for perennials to fill disappointing spots in the garden. For greenhouse owners there is more.

In January, as soon as the days start to lengthen, life begins again in the greenhouse. Apparently dead branches display the first signs of green. When the strengthening sun pushes the tempe-

rature to above 12° C during the day, the first green shoots appear. Fuchsia enthusiasts with a frost-free greenhouse can then enjoy the various winter-flowering fuchsia species and the cultivars developed from these. Just like the snowdrops and winter aconites in the winter garden, they are the messengers of spring. However cold and dark the winter may be, it forms the basis for a new spring. With that, our annual cycle is completed.

The winter rest

Although the fuchsias don't seem to need it, a break in the repotting, pruning, topping, watering, feeding and spraying, is very welcome for the gardener. Even the most fanatic fuchsia maniacs now have time to get their breath and get used to life without fuchsias. This can lead to contemplation. It is the Christmas season, a good book by the fire and a glass of wine around the Christmas tree. Fortunately, the fuchsia mania does not go so far that glass fuchsias are hung in the tree, but the wine can be made from fuchsia berries.

Collecting 'fuchsiana' or all kinds of objects decorated with fuchsias is fun, and the winter allows plenty of time for this. You then also have peace and quiet to study the new catalogues, which appear around the New Year, from national and foreign growers, and see if there is anything new.

'Danielle Frijstein' is a problem-free semi-trailer that can stand the heat well.

Perhaps it is the right time to decide whether or not you will become a member of a fuchsia association. That requires a well-considered decision, based on reliable information, because neither the club nor the member who leaves after one year because he is disappointed, gains from this situation. In addition of course, attention is needed for the overwintering plants. If they are in a trench or a freezer you can only wait and see, but if they are in the greenhouse or in the house, you will have to monitor the degree of moisture in the pot compost. When the frost sets in it becomes trickier. The difference between an excellent temperature for overwintering and irrevocably freezing to death is marginal.

'President Roosevelt' was a popular fuchsia 30 years ago. Now it is a forgotten, but excellent garden fuchsia.

Left: 'Fasnal 100'. Upright habit, light aubergine cultivar.

Below: 'Hermiena' is a good Dutch acquisition.

'Jans Veen' is a self-branching semi-trailer for semi-shade.

CHAPTER 4

Overwintering

Although some fuchsias are hardy, the majority are not. For the non-hardy plants a solution must be found to help them through the winter. They can, for example, live through the winter in a frost-free greenhouse, in the cellar or in a cold bedroom. Another alternative is to earth them in. You will read more about this in this chapter.

'Beacon Rosa' is a sport of 'Beacon', perhaps one of the best fuchsias we know.

Hardy fuchsias

In late spring it is time to give the hardy fuchsias their permanent place in the garden. Fuchsias in this part of the world are never really hardy, but with a bit of luck, in a not too exposed part of the garden and protected in winter by a 'blanket' of leaves or rough compost, they can dominate a border for years at a stretch with their elegance and constant flowering. At Castle Keukenhof in Lisse (Holland) there is a broad hedge of a *F. magellanica*-variety, which was planted around 1860. Every autumn the bushes are cut down and covered with a layer of beech leaves, and for nearly a century and a half they have been reappearing faithfully each spring. In mild winters it is even possible that the parts above

ground survive and make shoots in the spring. This is fairly normal in the milder climate of southern England and Ireland, where bushes can

Fuchsia magellanica *'Sharpitor' is probably a mutation of* F. magellanica *'Alba', one of the strongest hardy forms.*

Fuchsia regia ssp. regia *belongs, like* F. magellanica *to the* Quelusia *section. It is a wild grower which makes long liana-like branches up to 15 metres long in its area of spread.*

Fuchsia magellanica *'Aurea' is a golden coloured foliage sport of* F. magellanica.

'Chillerton Beauty' was introduced in 1847 and is still very popular.

Right: The green/gold foliage of 'Genii' at the end of the stem contrasts beautifully with the flowers.

grow metres tall and have stems over 10 cm thick.

The fuchsia literature is sometimes a little confusing. If it originates in England, the label 'hardy' does not apply everywhere. What in the South and West of the U.K. overwinters, does certainly not always apply to the North and East of Holland, for example. To overcome this, a project group from the Dutch circle of friends of the fuchsia (Nederlandse Kring van Fuchsia-vrienden) have tested various species and cultivars for hardiness.

The following positive results were obtained: *F. regia* (most sub species), *F. magellanica* (all varieties including 'Aurea', 'Sharpitor' and 'Variegata') , Beacon Rosa', Chillerton Beauty, 'Corallina', 'Display', 'Eva Boerg', 'Genii',

'Eva Boerg' is a strong garden plant.

'Lena' is a fuchsia for beginners. A spot in the open garden with a covering in winter is worth a try.

Left: 'Display'. A strongly upright fuchsia with beautifully-shaped flowers. One of the best garden-fuchsias which, with good protection, can survive outside, even in cold winters

Right: 'Amelie Aubin' is an elegant garden plant, which blooms profusely and makes few demands.

'Lena', 'Mercurius', 'Mrs W.P. Wood', 'Phyllis', 'Royal Purple', 'Saturnus', 'Whiteknight's Pearl' and 'White Pixie'. There are more, of course, and even more are being added thanks to the efforts of others including the Dutch hybridists.
Roughly it can be said that the light colours such as pink and white are quite rare and that there is no orange in the collection yet.

Planting hardy fuchsias
The end of May is the ideal time to give hardy fuchsias a spot in the garden as perennials. The risk of night frost, which could harm the new shoots, has then passed. There is now maximum time until the first frost of the next winter, by which time the plants will have had the best chance to settle down. It is important that the plant material consists of plants which are more than a year old.

A spring cutting has little chance of surviving the first winter. Therefore, when buying, always choose robust plants and, if you decide to work from cuttings, grow them in pots the first year and let them overwinter with the non-hardy fuchsias.

In his book, Gerrit van Veen promotes the idea of making a planting hollow of about 10 cm deep with a diameter of approx. 20 - 30 cm. He makes it in the loosened earth. In the hollow the actual plant hole is made in which the fuchsia is planted. In the course of the summer the fuchsia is, of course, usually earthed up. The

'Red Spider' is one of the better trailers.

desired effect of this method of working is that the part of the plant that must survive the frost, is well under the soil. The underground ends of the shoots can then sprout from a number of eyes the next year, producing a bushy plant.

It goes without saying that planting standards as hardy plants makes no sense. In a normal winter

the stem, and of course the crown, will almost certainly freeze to death.

Accommodation for the winter months

On the whole, fuchsias are not hardy. Sometimes they can survive the winter cold under ground, but it takes too much time then before they have recovered and start to bloom again. Nobody wants fuchsias if their first flowers appear in September on a measly little plant. Most cultivars don't even reach that and during a period of severe frost just die. Owners of carefully built-up collections certainly furiously hope to be able to go on the next year with the same collection. That's why all sorts of methods have been thought of to allow fuchsias to survive in this climate.

'Mercurius'. A hardy introduction from one of the first Dutch hybridists, Johan de Groot.

'Phyllis' needs a sunny location.

Whether or not fuchsias need a period of rest, is a point for discussion. Some react negatively to such an enforced break in growth and only survive the winter if they can go on growing at a pleasant temperature (above 12° C). In countries with a constant year-round frost-free climate it is clear that fuchsias only take a rest involuntarily. There are many though, which as 'long day' plants cease to bloom in the period when the days are shorter. Others, such as 'Machu Picchu', bloom in southern Australia continuously year in, year out.

The frost-free greenhouse

The frost-free greenhouse must be kept really frost-free. One night without heating during the

'White Pixie' is hardy in South-west Holland.

'Border Queen' is a strong garden plant for semi-shade.

'Royal Purple' is a robust problem-free upright cultivar with large flowers. Requires semi-shade.

'Paula Jane' is used by parks and gardens departments in flower tubs and beds.

frost period is fatal for many fuchsia plants, certainly for the younger ones. Personally I prefer double heating, to be certain, and not only

'WALZ Luit' is a striking trailing fuchsia which must go on growing during the winter.

Right: 'Saturnus' seen here growing in a fuchsia garden.

because, as a hybridist, I have unique specimens in my collection.

With oil or gas heating as the most important heat source and in addition a more expensive to run, thermostatically controlled electric greenhouse heater, nothing can really go wrong. Should the main heating fail, the electric heater can take over. You could of course dream up constructions in which an alarm goes off if the temperature drops too low.

As long as it doesn't freeze, there's no problem. The greenhouse can be ventilated during the day and when there is night frost an electric ventilator heater with a thermostat is enough to safeguard a temperature of approx. 5° C.

In addition, it is useful to hang a couple of maximum-minimum thermometers against the out-side wall.

If you check the temperature every morning and reset it, you can learn a lot about the behaviour of the temperature in your greenhouse. By the time it begins to get really cold, you know what measures to take. Keep an eye on the doors and windows because they easily develop chinks. You won't be the first person to leave a window open during heavy frost, by the way. As the winter progresses, the plants cautiously begin to make shoots, under the influence of higher temperatures during the day and, of course, the increasing light.

This process can be slowed down a bit, by a little judicious airing, if this is possible. If you really want more growth, then it is a good idea to raise the greenhouse temperature to 12° C. This

'WALZ Doedelzak' has flowers which are more curious than beautiful. It is a difficult plant in the winter.

only makes sense if you want to take early cuttings or are cultivating standards, for instance, or other unnatural shapes. Otherwise it is a waste of energy. Even with a lower greenhouse temperature, when all danger of night frost has

'WALZ Bella', in spite of the deviating name, belongs to the WALZ-musical instruments series.

'Lady Isobel Barnett' has an abundance of blooms and is suitable for shaping. It has outstanding flowers.

Fuchsias overwinter in sphagnum peat. The plants are eventually covered with sphagnum peat.

passed, around the middle of May, the plants will be developed far enough to go outside. There are, of course, fuchsias like the *triphylla* hybrids which are more sensitive to the cold or which have to go on growing through the winter to survive. This last category includes, apart from a number of species, the fuchsias with WALZ followed by the name of a musical instrument on the label. These WALZ-fuchsias are descendants of *F. magdalenae*, and, like *F. triphylla*,

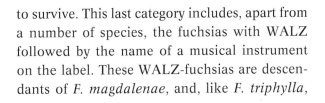

Fuchsias overwinter in sphagnum peat. The plants are bundled together and labelled well before storing.

'Präsident Walter Morio' is one of the latest Nutzinger acquisitions. It is a striking triphylla hybrid.

'Red Bells' is a vigorous upright cultivar with beautifully-shaped flowers.

Previous pages: 'Vobeglo' (grafted onto F.'Celia Smedley') grows much better on a strong rootstock. It is a beautiful but troublesome cultivar.

Below: 'Andenken an Heinrich Henkel' is a triphylla hybrid which can be used as a trailer in full sun.

this is a rather troublesome species. It is not wise to heat the whole greenhouse just for those few fuchsias. Fortunately, just below the roof of the greenhouse it is always warmer, because hot air rises. Put or hang those sensitive plants high in the greenhouse.

In order to waste as little as possible very expensive energy, it is advisable to insulate the greenhouse for the winter with blister padding. It takes away some light, but in the winter that is not so important. After the plants have been pruned – so that they don't take up so much space – they can be put into the greenhouse just as they are, next to each other. I like to have them outside for a couple of weeks after pruning. After cutting back, the still-active plants 'bleed' from the pruning wounds. That sap dries up nicely outside, but in the greenhouse it is a

'Berba's Fleur' is a good, upright garden variety.

'Golden Feli Fey' is a new introduction from Belgium which is not cultivated much as yet.

source of fungal infections. When pruning you must try to remove as much as possible of the green, the leaves and the branches which are still new wood. This green could be the cause of infecting the winter greenhouse population with all kinds of sap-sucking vermin and various

'Billy Green' likes a lot of light but is not really resistant to heat.

moulds like mildew and rust. In the spring in particular, a plague which begins in that way, rears its ugly head in no time. In the compost bin they can't do any more harm.

Although a frost-free greenhouse is the ideal place for overwintering your fuchsias, plenty of things can go wrong. Fuchsias which are buried in a trench have a much safer existence. Once the trench has been prepared in the right manner and filled, nothing can go wrong. Most fuchsias die in the winter through human error, and a greenhouse offers ample opportunity for this.

Trenching

In addition to allowing fuchsia plants to over-winter in a trench which has been dug, there are other methods, derived from this in which, for example, the fuchsias are 'potted up' in an old freezer. For both these methods the treatment of the plants is the same. Just as when they are prepared for the greenhouse, the fuchsias are first pruned back hard, mainly to save space. Don't however cut back into the old wood.

This does not make new shoots as easily as the young wood, from which at least two nodes must be left. After this, the plants are tapped out of their pots and the roots are rinsed bare. 'Nasties', such as the larvae of the vine weevil, are largely

disposed of at this stage. Then an indelible name-tag is attached to the stem with strong twine. In the meantime you have dug the trench to a safe depth above the water level which can be expected in a wet winter. You can gain depth here, by raising the edges of the trench using part of the dug-out soil. You then lay the plants in the trench on a bed of lightly-dampened sphagnum peat, so that the stems and the bushes are lying flat. A branch which has overwintered lying flat makes better shoots in the spring. After a layer of plants, make a layer of sphagnum peat, and so on. It is enough to fill the trench to within 10 cm

Left: Fuchsia 'Radings Gerda' is an encliandra-*hybrid from Drude Reiman. She introduced all 'Radings'-cultivars.*

Right: 'WALZ Waterval' is a profusely-flowering trailer for semi-shade and does not tolerate heat.

Below: 'Display' looks like Frau Ida Noack.

from the top. Then lay a plank over the trench, leaving at least 10 cm air space under it. Cover the plank with plastic foil and then cover this with about 20 cm of earth. The trench is then finished and you won't need to worry about it until next year.

Over the years it has been demonstrated that 20 cm earth and 10 cm of air space is sufficient insulation for moderate frost. In a freezer or other kind of well-insulated container the

Left: 'Caspar Hauser' is very striking through its unusual corolla colour. The German hybridist Wilfried Springer made a name for himself with this acquisition.

Right: 'Cloth of Gold' is a somewhat weaker cultivar with striking foliage colour.

Below: 'Frau Ida Noach' is very similar to 'Display' and is a good and more or less hardy fuchsia.

method is the same. This solution saves you heavy groundwork and, because the container stays in the shed or garage, there is more room left in the garden for planting bulbs.

When there is severe frost, it is wise to give the container extra protection with blankets or blister foil.

The trench method is, in view of rising energy prices, an excellent method for overwintering, certainly as far as getting the stronger fuchsia cultivars through the winter. Many of the more unusual species and their descendants, such as

Left: 'Multa' is a semi-trailer with strongly-contrasting, rather small flowers. It requires some shelter.

Right: 'Glitters' is an excellent upright growing cultivar in orange-red shades.

Below: 'Postiljon' is a charming trailing fuchsia from the Dutch hybridist Van der Post.

'Mantilla' is one of the most beautiful cultivars. In the winter this plant often gives problems.

triphylla hybrids, do not tolerate this treatment. The ever-recurring problem with trenches is: what to do with the plants in the spring to get them in good condition for the garden in the middle of May?

The semi-permanent greenhouse

Handy enthusiasts solved this problem long ago by building a sort of tent out of plastic foil and some support material in little-used places in the garden, where fuchsias could be brought on in the early spring, when there was only a bit of night frost.

These days, various suppliers of gardening accessories have taken advantage of this. They offer tunnel-like plastic greenhouses, which are inexpensive and can be set up or taken down in no time at all. These semi-permanent greenhouses, for which there is generally no need for planning permission, can bridge the gap for enthusiasts with large collections of fuchsias or

other tub plants. If it threatens to be a cold night, it is easy to place a simple electric ventilator which is sufficient to prevent frost damage to new green shoots.

'Schweitzer Grusz' is a little-known Austrian introduction. Its outward appearance, however, does not tally with the described triphylla *origin.*

It is very important to air these greenhouses if the weather permits. If it stays damp – a disadvantage of this type of greenhouse – then serious damage from grey mould (*Botrytis cinerea*) will almost certainly be the result. Airing, even if only to keep the greenhouse temperature within reasonable limits when the sun shines and which has to be done in ordinary greenhouses anyway, makes the transition to outside a bit easier.

The cold frame

If you have a modest collection of fuchsias, consisting of plants which are not too tall, you can easily use a cold frame.

Traditionally this comprised a wooden or brick frame – higher at the back than at the front – on

Left: 'Cambridge Louie' is a good show plant with slightly outstanding flowers.

Below: 'Cross Check' is a good semi-trailer which needs to be topped hard.

which single panes of glass rested. Weather permitting, these panes of glass were opened during the day, supported by a brick. During night frosts rush matting was rolled out over them to prevent too much heat loss.

Nowadays, frames of aluminium and glass can be bought. Blister foil can replace the rush mats, and has the advantage that on cold days the plants get enough light. The advantage of cold frames is that the plants can stay in them until they are fully hardened off.

Overwintering indoors

Since most houses now have central heating and no cellar, it is difficult to find a suitable place in the house for overwintering. Allowing fuchsias to overwinter in the house is always an emergency measure.

There is always the problem that the air is too dry, which is not solved even by spraying the plants regularly with water. In addition, it is too warm in our houses. A warm overwintering place causes the plant to begin to grow again, thus needing more light, which is scarce in the winter. Attics where pelargoniums overwinter successfully year after year, are usually too dry, too warm and too dark for fuchsias. A spare bedroom in which the radiator is only turned on when it really freezes, is usually the best bet. However, necessity is the mother of invention. I know of cases in which the plants are kept in the crawling space under a house, or even in dustbin bags filled with damp sphagnum peat under the bed in a cold bedroom.

If you are fortunate enough to have a cellar, things are a quite a bit better for you, unless of course the central heating boiler is located there.

Right: 'Stella Ann' is a striking, light-coloured triphylla *hybrid. Give it full sun in the summer and keep it in the greenhouse in the winter.*

Below: 'Happy' is, as the name suggests, a real dwarf. It is suitable for edging.

'Son of Thumb'. This sport from 'Tom Thumb' is hardy in a sheltered spot.

Cellars are cool, frost-free and usually moderately damp.

Only the light is a problem. By burning a couple of 'Grow-Lux' fluorescent lamps above the plants, this problem is easily solved. It uses some electricity of course, but the costs are negligible compared to the cost of energy for keeping the greenhouse frost-free.

The (principally blue) light from these lamps ensures that the developing young shoots are a normal shape and colour. They otherwise develop long, thin yellowish-white strings, which are not even suitable for use as cuttings. These stringy specimens are extra vulnerable to pests like red spider mite, whitefly and aphids, and long to be out in the open air.

Fuchsias which have overwintered in cellars and crawling spaces should really be treated like plants which have been in trenches. Fuchsias which have come through the winter in a frost-free, light place in the attic or on the windowsill of a cool room are best compared to those from a frost-free greenhouse, albeit that climatological circumstances are better in the greenhouse. Most fuchsia plants indoors are afflicted by shortage of light, dry air and almost always a temperature which is too high.

In our grandmother's time, when our houses were still heated by coal fires, it was still possible to cultivate fuchsias on the windowsill.

In centrally-heated houses this is difficult. Even in the lightest places – which mustn't be too sunny – they grow weak and stringy. If there are not too many plants it's best to leave them outside. As long as it doesn't freeze they are best left in a sheltered spot. Of course that means paying a lot of attention to weather forecasts, because one forgotten night frost could cause a lot of damage.

After the danger of frost has passed

Wherever a fuchsia-lover keeps his plants, he longs for the moment when his plants can go into the garden. After the traditional cold period in late spring, the chance of serious night frost is quite small.

If there is a light ground frost, it is usually sufficient to cover the plants with newspaper,

'Brodsworth' is a shrub for semi-shade. It strongly resembles the mother plant, 'Mrs Popple' and is possibly hardy too.

plastic sheeting or, even better, with acrylic fleece at night to prevent damage. The usually reasonably accurate weather forecasts for the coming five days, give timely warning of a serious risk of frost.

While almost everyone is worried about the risk of night frosts when bringing out their plants, another possibly even greater danger is forgotten - burning by the sun. Fuchsias which are taken straight from the protective greenhouse climate and stood in the sun with a cutting wind, run the risk of losing all their leaves through sunburn. This is more damaging than a little bit of night frost.

Fuchsias, but also other plants, protect themselves from radiation from the sun, by making reddish pigments. Just as we must expose our skin gradually to sunlight, so must plants have time to build up their protection. If there is enough room, the fuchsia plants are best acclimatised in light shade; from trees for example. If this is not possible, screens can solve the problem. Personally, I hang a collection of trailing fuchsias directly on the pergola in my front garden which has little shade, but for the first three weeks I hang a screen above them. The screen is only removed when the weather report forecasts cloudy skies for the coming days.

'Golden La Campanella' is a beautiful leaf-sport of 'La campanella', one of the nicest semi-trailers. It often has over-wintering problems and is identical to 'Princess Pot.

CHAPTER 5

Watering, feeding and repotting

Plants usually consist of more than 80% water, but there is more needed to keep them healthy. With the aid of water and carbon dioxide the plant can produce all kinds of sugars, including our ordinary sugar, starch and cellulose, and not forgetting glucose. Carbon dioxide is obtained from the air through the stomata and we don't have to worry about that. For the production of proteins more is involved.

Plants can make these from glucose and salts. These salts dissolved in water are usually absorbed by the roots. To ensure that the ground always contains enough salts, we have to provide these in the form of fertiliser.

'Göttingen', a triphylla hybrid, is often used in Holland as a parent for crossing.

Watering

Generally speaking, the plants outside will need less water than those in the greenhouse, as long as the weather is not really hot. Overwatering of weakly specimens in particular can lead to their demise at this time.

Too little water can do no harm for once, but it does mean more work. The most frequently used composts for fuchsias contain a lot of peat and a ball of peat shrinks as it dries and loosens itself from the pot.

Just watering in the normal way is pretty useless because the water simply runs away along the sides of the earth. The only solution is to dip the plant in water with a dash of washing-up

'Oriënt Express' is a striking introduction from the English hybridist Edwin Goulding. He called a number of his products of the crossings after famous trains.

'Leverkusen' is a good triphylla hybrid for bonsai-culture. Great differences in temperature often cause the buds and flowers to fall off.

'Brighton Belle' flowers early, profusely and long in a sunny spot.

liquid added to it. As far as the water quality is concerned, fuchsias are fortunately not very difficult. Soft water containing little dissolved salts is the best choice. Rainwater seems to be the best option in many cases, but unfortunately there can be local heavy chemical pollution in this.

Although fuchsias like to have a slightly acid soil, sometimes the rainwater is more like inorganic acid, which for watering is a bit too much of a good thing. Water from ditches and groundwater provide the cheapest solution.

Many enthusiasts will have to make do with tap-water though. Where the water is very hard –contains a lot of salts–, it is wise to be careful about the dosage of soluble fertilisers. If there is a high salt content in the soil ball in the pot, which includes the salts in the fertiliser, the roots are less able to absorb water.

In the worst cases they even die off and the plant is doomed. This can also happen through over-watering because then the oxygen, which the roots need to be able to function, is driven out of the ground.

Watering tub plants

For all plants in pots and tubs, dosing the water is the most difficult task. Too little water is the lesser of two evils, even though it inhibits successful growth, especially if it goes so far that the fine hair-roots and the even finer root hairs dry out. The plant then has to make new ones and that takes time. Too much water is often deadly.

The air is thereby forced out of the pot ground and the roots suffocate in the mud. The plant droops and the only thing you can do is swiftly take a few cuttings and save what you can. For fuchsias there is fortunately a lot of leeway between too much and too little water. As long as you stay within this, not much can go wrong. Don't be tempted to give more water during hot days when the plants are drooping, although the pot-ground is still moist.

It is better to spray the surroundings; by doing this the plants can revive in a cooler, moister environment. How damp the soil ball really is, can best be tested by weighing the pot on your hand. The colour of the soil surface also gives an indication.

Watering can or spray

If there are only a few plants, it's best to use an ordinary watering can, preferably one with a

'Brighton Belle' flowers early, profusely and long in a sunny spot.

'Elfriede Ott' is a strong well-branching semi-trailer.

long thin spout. The advantage of a watering can is that the water can be brought up to temperature beforehand and if necessary a measured amount of fertiliser can be added.

For larger collections the garden hose is usually used. This can be connected to the water supply or a pump for pond water or groundwater. There are devices on sale which can, if fitted between the tap and the spray nozzle, add fertiliser to the water. Overfeeding through uneven assimilation of the fertiliser is certainly risky, especially with the cheaper equipment.

The spraying itself can be done with a spray-gun, which is adjustable from coarse to very fine. To water trailers or pots placed deep into the borders, a hose fitted onto the gun, preferably with a slightly bent nozzle, is very convenient.

Dripping

For a really large collection I advise the drip method, certainly if they are hanging pots. For the DIY'er there are complete irrigation sets in the shops, with or without an adjustable automatic control. Even watering computers can be supplied, which, with the aid of sensors, work on the humidity of the soil in the pot.

It is cheaper, however, to make a made-to-measure irrigation system of black polyethylene tubing with holes punched in it and thin tubes of the same material fixed into the holes. These tubes are pushed into each pot with a plastic

coffee stirrer or with adjustable droppers. A system of this kind can easily serve more than a hundred pots with water at the same time. I water my trailers like this once a day in the summer until the water drips out under the pots. In the colder seasons it is better to water by hand only where necessary. In the summer it doesn't matter so much and the drip method saves a lot of time and work. It is necessary to monitor this of course. Because tubes can get blocked, plants can dry out and through too much water a weaker plant can drown. When using drip irrigation with droppers which cannot be adjusted, it is best to use pots of the same size. A combination of drop-irrigation and semi-hydroculture is ideal, because with this method any water surplus can run away and there is always a water reserve.

'Steirerblut' is a recent acquisition from Austria with a triphylla origin. It needs sun and warmth.

Semi-hydroculture

To prevent the soil ball drying out, particularly in the summer, without being forced to water several times a day, you could choose for a method known as semi-hydroculture. Hanging pots especially, lose a great deal of water during hot, sunny weather. The soil ball can dry out so severely that only protracted immersion in water with a few drops of washing-up liquid can bring any solace. The soap reduces the surface tension, by which moisture absorption is increased. In principle, every plastic pot can be made suitable for hydro-culture.

Usually the so-called Danish pots are used, however. The existing drainage holes in the bottom of the pots are first blocked off with waterproof sticky tape. Then new drainage holes are drilled or melted in the sides of the pot about

'Estelle Marie' is a beautiful, shade-loving erect flowering cultivar, suitable as a bedding plant.

The fuchsias are watered.

3 cm up from the bottom. To make the holes, a simple soldering iron with a round end works perfectly. The pot is then filled up as far as the holes with granules of baked clay. On top of this comes a well-fitting piece of gauze. You can cut this out of plastic insect screen, available everywhere. You then fill the pot up with potting compost.

Plants in this kind of pot always have a water supply at their disposal while the soil kept drained. The gauze ensures that the clay granules are kept separate, and can be disinfected and re-used for repotting. A good-sized piece of 'oasis' in the bottom of the pot can likewise serve the same purpose as moisture reserve.

Watering during the winter

In the winter, due to lack of space, fuchsias often stand close together. Every corner of the greenhouse is in use. This creates a rather cluttered situation which is fatal to the proper manner of watering. Most of the victims fall to overwatering. Seldom do they dry out.

If in doubt, don't water. On the other hand, in the second half of the winter, when the fuchsias want to start growing again, a lightly moist soil ball is necessary.

The problem of watering is now re-opened. It can do no harm, if the weather is sunny, to spray the plants lightly with water. Make sure there is enough ventilation if you do this, by opening windows and, if possible, running a fan.

High humidity and stagnant air can cause severe damage through botrytis.

Feeding

By the time we put our fuchsias outside, a lot of the fertiliser in the pot compost will have been used up. Since fuchsias have to perform vigorously in a short period of growth, it is wise to begin giving extra food. The simplest method for this is to strew granules of organic fertiliser regularly onto the compost in the pot.

This organic fertiliser is on sale in various compositions. The advantage of organic fertiliser is that the nutritious elements are released gradually, so that the chance of overfeeding is not as great. The use of soluble fertiliser during watering is a widely-used alternative. It requires more effort in general because it has to be done more often, since the dosage is critical.

Never give more fertiliser than the amount recommended on the packet. That is asking for trouble, particularly with pot plants.

Composition of fertiliser

Fertiliser for pot plants is composed of nitrogen compounds(N), phosphorus (P) and potassium (K). In addition to this, an all-round mixture also contains trace elements such as magnesium (Mg) and iron (Fe). Nitrogen, in particular, has influence on the plant growth. Phosphorus encourages root growth and stimulates flowering, together with potassium, which also heightens the intensity of the flower colour. Magnesium is necessary for the formation of chlorophyll. The N-P-K composition is generally shown on the packaging of the plant food: 20-20-20 means that a fertiliser contains 20% nitrogen, 20% phosphorus and 20% po-tassium and, in addition, should contain trace elements.

'Margaret Pilkington' is an easy-growing upright cultivar, profusely flowering.

'Groenekan's Glorie' is a Dutch introduction from the nursery-man Stevens from Groenekan near Hilversum.

For fuchsias this is an acceptable year-round composition. And yet, some growers like to give some extra phosphorus to young plants in the spring for better rooting: 10-52-10 is then quite usual. In spring too, a composition with the ratio of 28-14-14 is sometimes used. Through the higher dose of nitrogen the plants grow faster. Fuchsias are usually fed with fertiliser once a week. It is, however, better to give one seventh of the weekly dose in the daily watering. In this way the supply to the plant is more stable, and less unused fertiliser is washed out. In addition to the mistake of giving the plants a higher dose of fertiliser than is advised, there is also the misconception that plants which are looking sickly, can be saved with an extra dose. It is better to put such plants in a smaller pot with fresh compost and then put them carefully in a place out of the sun to try to get them going

again. Never give more fertiliser than stated on the packaging. If you are pleased with the fertiliser you are using, don't let seeing plants growing more beautifully on a different fertiliser regime tempt you into another method of feeding. In principle, all fertilisers contain the same salts, so what's the point? Never try to push plants which are not doing so well with extra fertiliser. Enough is as good as a feast!

Organic fertiliser

Organic fertiliser originates from dead organisms, mostly plants which have been consumed by animals, bacteria or fungi. This is a natural process which, for example, keeps forests fertile. For a large part, the organic fertiliser on sale in shops is made of animal droppings.

Cow manure is very suitable, but so is garden worm manure. Pig and chicken manure is too strong to be used on pot plants when it is fresh, but horse manure is eminently suitable.

In addition to these organic fertilisers, which include blood and bonemeal, compost is a good source of food for plants. Organic domestic waste makes excellent fertiliser and has a structure which can improve the soil.

Bacteria and fungi break this refuse down gradually into the original constituents. During this process, so much heat is released that harmful organisms, and in many cases even weed

'Cliff's Own' has jaunty little flowers in an unusual colour combination. It is a bushy plant for semi-shade.

'Golondrina' is a striking fuchsia, which is hardy in England.

seeds, are destroyed. Organic fertiliser is the most easily applied in granules. Once in three weeks a full teaspoonful per two-litre pot gives a fair idea of the dosage. In a damp environment, fungus sometimes forms on the granules. This fungus is absolutely harmless to the plants and even enables the fertiliser to be absorbed more rapidly.

The most important advantage of organic fertilising is that the nutritional elements, the salts, enter the ground more gradually. In this way, there is less risk of overfeeding.

Inorganic fertiliser

Although it is a pity to use artificial fertiliser produced by the chemical industry, when we have a surplus of manure, the former has certain advantages in use.

Particularly if you want to steer the development of plants by giving them more of certain chemicals, you have no other choice. Artificial fertiliser dissolved in water can also be used for foliar feeding. If the water you are using already contains a lot of unusable salts, feeding can also be given via the foliage, thus preventing the salt content of the soil from becoming excessive, without the plant suffering from malnutrition. A good fertiliser for fuchsias in the summer has an N-P-K ratio of 20-20-20.

If you want faster growth, you can use, for instance, sodium nitrate, calcium nitrate or the rather slower-working ammonium sulphate, to give some extra nitrogen. Extra phosphorus to stimulate flowering can be given in the form of super phosphate or Thomas basic slag. For more potassium to intensify the flower colour for instance, you can give potassium nitrate. The disadvantage of all these forms of fertiliser is that, dissolved in water, they get into the ground in high concentrations almost immediately after use.

Over-fertilising is a real danger and the fertiliser which is washed out, means an extra burden on the environment. The problems of over-fertilising can be prevented by using resin-coated fertiliser granules.

The nutritional salts gradually seep through this resin coating spread over a longer period – up to nine months. In general a higher ground temperature hastens that process, just as the plants are growing faster.

Fertiliser in the winter

Feeding is usually not necessary in the winter months. The plants have just been repotted anyway, and have fresh nutritious potting compost at their disposal, or they will get fresh compost at the beginning of spring. By the time the plants begin to be well in leaf, it can, of course, do no harm to use foliar feeding to make up possible shortages.

Repotting

Since fuchsias in pots and tubs have to perform well every year, it is worthwhile renewing the ground from which they must get their food, either wholly or partly, every growing season. Through watering with water which is often too rich in lime and feeding with all kinds of artificial fertiliser, the pot compost changes too. Even the structure of the potting compost can change for the worse in the course of the growing season by, for example, becoming too compact. Compact ground soon has too little air to provide the roots with sufficient oxygen. Repotting is then really a necessary operation every year.

Plants which have overwintered without a soil ball, for example trenched in, must of course be repotted with fresh potting compost. Plants which have retained their soil ball can be planted into a larger pot or in a pot of the same size after the soil ball has been thoroughly shaken out and, where necessary, root pruning has been done. For the actual repotting the pot is partially filled with potting compost. On top of this comes the plant. The pot is subsequently filled to just under the rim. This leaves room for watering so that the water doesn't run away over

the edge of the pot. By tapping the pot, the compost fills up the spaces between the roots. Finally the plant is gently firmed and watered. Never put repotted plants directly into a sunny place. After repotting, new roots with root hairs must first be formed in order to ensure water transport for the water balance in the plant.

When to repot?

Particularly in the spring, when the fuchsia plants still have few leaves and a strong urge towards regrowth, this operation can be carried out without damage. There are, however, those who favour repotting after the growing season, just before or during the winter. This has the important advantage that larvae of the dreaded

'Pink Jade' shows a striking combination of pink and green. It is an upright bush for semi-shade.

'Marloesje ter Beek'. A charming name for a charming little flower that looks like 'Keukenhof', among others. It probably comes from Holland.

'Duke of York' is an excellent garden plant with flowers of the classic type and red-veined yellow-green foliage.

vine weevil which may be present, can be caught before they have destroyed the plant during the winter season by eating through the roots.

Potting compost

Many enthusiasts used to make their own potting compost. Some older books on fuchsias give extensive recipes for making it.

Nowadays it is not unusual in a garden centre to find all sorts of potting composts for the most diverse plant species. Even when the range is limited, fuchsia compost is nearly always present. The most important component is generally some kind of peat.

In view of the fact that fertilisers have been added to this compost, it is unnecessary to feed the plants yourself for the first six weeks. I personally prefer potting compost which also contains some clay. A mixture of this sort tends to shrink less when it is dry. The addition of composted tree bark also has roughly the same effect and makes the ground somewhat lighter in structure for a longer time.

I strongly advise against the use of old soil, supplemented by organic fertiliser or garden compost. Such mixtures often have a salt content which is too high. The ground could also be infected with organisms which are harmful to fuchsias.

Pots and tubs

In the choice of pots and tubs personal taste and the size of your bank account play an important part. Nobody would deny that earthenware pots and wooden tubs are very beautiful, but housing a large collection in these is very pricey.

Fuchsia-lovers usually choose for black plastic pots. They are cheap, light in use, easily available in all possible shapes and sizes and after use are easy to clean and store. Other colours, such as white, are just like those in the terracotta colour, a bit 'kitschy'.

If you do choose for terra-cotta, it's best to use the traditional earthenware pots. For hanging pots, black is unfortunately an un-favourable colour. Where they are exposed to sun, they absorb so much heat that the roots, which for the greater part touch the inside wall of the pot, are almost 'cooked'. Inside insulation of the pot, with a layer of thin blister padding for instance, solves this problem.

It is also possible to work with an outer pot which is a little wider. The air space between the inner and outer pot forms efficient insulation.

Which size pot?

Generally speaking the pot for a fuchsia should not be too large. The legendary fuchsia grower Jim Travis used to say that you shouldn't put a small child into an adult-sized bed. Young cuttings certainly have initially enough room in a pot 9 cm in diameter. By the time there is a definite root system on the outside of the soil ball - tap the plant out of the pot and have a look - the plant is put into a larger pot.

By repeating the repotting a few times during growth, the soil ball will have a root system which is not only on the outside. The absorption of water and food will then also function better. Some fuchsia cultivars, such as 'Lady's Smock' and 'WALZ Kattesnor' and species such as *F. triphylla*, have a very vulnerable root system. In a pot which is too large they will sometimes not be able to absorb a possible excess of water quickly. The consequence could be that the compost becomes muddy and the roots die off through lack of oxygen. For these weaker plants take a smaller pot size and a light compost

mixture, with 30% cocopeat for example. As fuchsia plants get larger they naturally demand more spacious accommodation for their root systems. For a good-sized plant you should allow for a minimum pot content of 2 litres. If you have enough space to allow really big plants to overwinter, you can cultivate these in 200 litre tubs. Fuchsia bushes and standards grown in tubs like this can really demonstrate what a fast-growing cultivar can achieve.

Specimens with a crown diameter of several metres and of corresponding height are absolutely no exception.

'Northway'. For good results an extra dose of nitrogen in the spring is recommended.

CHAPTER 6

Propagating fuchsias

Fuchsias have probably become so popular because they are so simple to propagate. A young shoot, cut off in March, can be blooming nicely in August. Most fuchsia-lovers certainly have plenty of material for cuttings in the spring, because the plants have to be topped. The true enthusiast plants these cuttings and gives them away to friends and neighbours or passers-by.

Many people have become infected with 'fuchsia madness' in this way. Propagating from seed is another matter. Most cultivated fuchsias are the products of crossings and that means that they may not remain true to type. Their offspring, cultivated from seed, display a hotch potch of shapes and colours, although single red/purple will dominate most seeds. Since our culture fuchsias have originated through directed crossing and careful selection by experts, it is not likely that seeds just winkled out of a few berries or from a bought packet of seeds, will produce novelties which are anything like worthwhile. The wild species are more or less true to type. That sometimes makes it worthwhile to propagate by seed which must though be obtained by controlled self-pollination. There are namely species from which it is very difficult to take cuttings.

'Die schöne Wilhelmine' is a striking modern acquisition from the German grower Springer.

Taking cuttings in the spring

'New Market' is possibly identical to 'Brilliant'. It is a good fuchsia for a sunny position.

The simplest way to take a cutting is to take a young shoot about 10 cm long, from which the bottom pair of leaves has been cut away with a sharp knife, and stand it in a little bottle of water. Within a couple of weeks at the most, roots will have formed and the cutting can be potted up. This method shows very clearly that the roots appear chiefly at the joint.

Unfortunately, the roots of a water cutting do not function in the ground. New roots first have to be made before further growth can occur. That is why growers and experienced fuchsia-lovers put cuttings straight into the ground. This usually works very well in the general potting composts suitable for fuchsias. It is, of course, even better to use special striking medium, which contains fewer nutrients.

Potting compost is similar to this, with, for example, some sharp sand or cocopeat mixed through it to lower the nutritional value and create a somewhat lighter soil structure. Cuttings strike best in the spring. The plants are then totally geared to their vegetative development, which means that they not only produce nice young shoots, suitable for cuttings, but also that the shoots root easily.

'Sophie's Surprise' should have variegated foliage - that was the surprise. The photo shows a 'reverted' plant which is identical to the original mutated cultivar 'Sophie Claire'.

The grower plants the cuttings, which just at that time are cut in large numbers from the 'mother plants', in pots or plastic multi-pot trays. After the bottom leaves have been removed, the cuttings are first dipped in rooting powder and then put into planting holes which have been made in the compost. Then the compost is lightly firmed around the cutting. In the propagator with bottom heat of about 20° C both plant and compost are kept moist. Unfortunately, this environment is also ideal for other things, including grey mould (botrytis). It is therefore wise, especially if the cuttings are close to each other, to spray everything well with a fungicide. On a smaller scale, fuchsia cuttings strike very well in small flowerpots which are each placed in a plastic lunch bag.

When the cuttings begin to grow, first open the bag at the top. By gradually sliding the plastic

Here you can see this from close by.

Then the bottom leaves are cut off.

Subsequently the stem is cut off below a leaf bud.

To take a cutting a top cutting is first cut off.

bag down in the following days, the cuttings, which have rooted in the meantime, can acclimatise to the dryer outside air.

Naturally there are all sorts of indoor greenhouses and even electrically heated propagators, which offer more luxurious opportunities. It is always important to keep the cuttings out of the sun and give them sufficient water. Fallen leaves or other dead material must be removed regularly, because this provides an ideal medium for fungus damage.

When spring is over and the fuchsia plants enter their flowering phase, taking cuttings is not so easy. It usually succeeds, but the use of rooting powder is then a must. The plant hormones, which are present in this and stimulate rooting, are only made by the plant in sufficient measure in the spring. In the summer they make principally growth substances which encourage flowering and seed-formation.

Raising cuttings

Once the cuttings have rooted, they must be potted on. It can be useful to top them at the

'Hobson's Choice'. Hobson's choice is certainly not my choice. This cultivar tolerates sun.

Write the name of the cultivar on a label.

The cutting is dipped into rooting powder.

A planting hole is made.

same time, so that the young plants start to branch at once. If you want to grow a standard, however, topping is forbidden for the time being. The cutting must grow on, without branching until it reaches the desired height.

To this end, all sideshoots are pinched out at an early stage. When the desired height has been

The cutting is planted in the hole.

The cuttings are put under plastic.

After pricking out, the cuttings look like this.

reached, the young whip is stopped. With the aid of the sideshoots, which grow from the top two or three leaf axils, the crown can subsequently be formed.

Most fuchsia cultivars have two leaves per joint and also form two sideshoots in the axils of these. Sometimes, however, shoots grow with wreaths of three leaves per joint. Cuttings from

such shoots are ideal for making standards, since they produce 50% more branches to form the crown with. For young fast-growing plants in small pots, it is worth employing foliar-feeding. Certainly in areas where the water already contains many salts, dying as a consequence of a too-high salt concentration in the ground can be prevented.

Propagation in the autumn

Nobody wants to have more plants to care for in the winter. And yet it is handy to take cuttings from the more difficult fuchsia cultivars and species before the winter.

Sometimes they can tolerate winter conditions better as young plants. Even a popular cultivar

'Harry Gray' is a double, almost white, semi-trailer.
It grows well in semi-shade. It can give problems with
overwintering.

Fuchsia arborescens. *The frosted berry clusters have great decorative value.*

like 'La Campanella' has more difficulty in getting through the winter as a mature plant than as an autumn-struck cutting. This applies in even greater measure to its descendants and, for example, the magnificent *triphylla* hybrid 'Mantilla'. Some species, *F. excorticata* for instance, propagate more easily from hardwood cuttings than from softwood cuttings. It is also attractive via this method to lay the basis for new plants in the spring. There is plenty of wood available from pruning.

In autumn the fuchsia berries ripen of course. If you have a lot of them, it's worth making jam, but only if you haven't used systemic control pesticides. I even once had a present of fuchsia berry wine, so what's stopping you?

The fruits of pollinated flowers, which have a label around the stem, are carefully collected for the seed harvest.

They contain the most exciting ingredient for the 'fuchsia fun' of the hybridist.

'Fiona' (plaited stem). When the buds open, the sepals remain stuck together at the point, which gives a lantern-like effect.

Right: 'Die Schöne Wilhelmine' is beautiful as a bush, but is really ideal to cultivate as a bonsai.

'Mantilla'. For this cultivar, a plant of this size is rare.

Autumn cuttings

The fuchsia specialist Leo B. Boullemier, who is sadly no longer with us, taught me a good method for taking autumn cuttings. When he became older he no longer had a greenhouse.

The small collection of fuchsias he still kept, overwintered as cuttings. To do this, he struck them in small pots, using rooting powder and fungicide. He placed each pot on the screw top lid of, say an instant coffee jar. After having made the cutting and the compost nicely moist, he screwed the jar, minus its label of course, back onto the pot. In these mini-greenhouses his entire collection survived the winter without him having to lift a finger.

These 'propagating jars' need to be in a light, not too cold place, without sun. The method can be adapted to the circumstances of course, but the principle is ideal.

Wood cuttings

Anton Bremer, a prominent member of the Dutch Circle of Fuchsia Friends (NKVF), an enthusiastic experimenter with wide experience, once developed this method of striking fuchsia

'Flowerdream' really is a dream in an attractive colour combination from the Dutch hybridist Martin Rijff. Protect it from wind and sun.

cuttings. It is a method much used in tree and shrub nurseries.

For this he used the approx. 10 cm long thick bottom ends of branches which were formed in the same year and were now wooded and pruned back before the winter storage. He kept them in a cool frost-free place in lightly damp, sharp sand or sphagnum peat. Not until early spring was rooting considered. For the actual cuttings, a piece of about 1 cm is cut from the bottom with a good, sharp knife. The new ends are then dampened and dipped into a mixture of rooting powder and fungicide powder 1:1. They are then put back upside down into the peat mull, so that the powdered section sticks out. After standing in a cool place for three days, they are transferred to high, transparent jars, where they are stood loosely on a couple of centimetres of potting medium. After it has all been moistened the pots are covered with plastic foil. With bottom heat from a radiator, on a windowsill protected from the sun for instance, they root within a couple of weeks. Young shoots also appear then, sometimes it is best to use those shoots as cuttings to get well-shaped plants.

For the other method, the wood cuttings should be potted up when the roots are only a few centimetres long. A great number of the new Dutch fuchsia cultivars in the U.S.A. arrived as wood cuttings. Vegetable material in soil is not

'Pluto' is hardy in Southern England.

Below: 'Azure Sky'. The blue/lilac colour of the corolla alas disappears shortly after the bud opens. The name is probably wishful thinking.

admitted into the U.S.A., but for small bunches of fuchsia twigs there is no problem in getting a health certificate for America.

'Carillon van Amsterdam'. An acquisition from the Dutch grower Van Wieringen. This fuchsia gets forgotten because of its 'ordinary' colour.

'Mood Indigo'. One of the many 'Rosae' descendants from Herman de Graaff. This absolute eye-catcher is very floriferous, but in stages.

Seed

In the course of autumn, the fruits, which are the results of crossing work in late summer, indicate their ripeness by colouring. There are great differences in that area. Normal fuchsia berries are dark red in colour when ripe, but there are those which remain greenish although they are ripe. Other colours are intensely dark pink, almost black and even orange. Such colours are only found in species and then only in their direct offspring. A ripe fuchsia berry becomes soft and then falls off. For the seed harvest it is better to pick them before they fall off. Otherwise you don't know where they will fall. It can also be useful to protect them from greedy birds. Some blackbirds soon discover that the

'Anna of Longleat' is an upright cultivar with an abundance of semi-double blooms, provided it is well topped. It is a good English acquisition from 1985 which requires semi-shade.

exotic fuchsia berries are delicious. To obtain the seed, the berry is squashed onto a piece of paper – a paper towel for example. The seeds are then visible and can be extracted from the fruit pulp with the help of a dissecting needle. Since only the round seeds are germinative, the flat

Above: 'Rose of Castile' is eminently suitable to grow as a large solitairy plant in a tub.

'Other Fellow' is an easy, upright growing fuchsia with blooms in a rare colour combination.

'Rose of Castile' has not been a popular fuchsia since 1855 without reason. The photo clearly shows the difference in crown colour when the bloom is fading.

specimens can be rejected. A magnifying glass such as those used for embroidery, with a built-in lamp, can be very useful in this selection work, because fuchsia seeds, which look rather like grape pips, are sometimes very tiny. Direct sowing is the easiest way, but since winter is coming and the young seedlings would then suffer light-deficiency, it is wiser to wait until January. Fuchsia seed stored in a paper bag in a cool, dry place can keep its germinative power for months.

Cultivation from seed

Since fuchsia seed usually involves small numbers per crossing, it is better to use small trays to avoid mixing species. The round, transparent, small plastic dishes, in which nuts, salads, etc. are sold, are often used for sowing. These dishes

Following pages: 'Jean Ewart', named after a former president of the British Fuchsia Society, is a good plant for semi-shade.

have a diameter of approx. 10 cm and are suitable for about 50 seeds. Even if they all germinate, there is enough space for the plants until they are pricked out.

A layer of 2 - 3 cm of sowing compost goes onto the bottom of the dish. Special seed compost is available, but for fuchsias ordinary potting compost can also be used, with or without the addition of cocopeat (composted coconut fibre) to make the sowing medium a little lighter. This fibrous structure also works better for pricking out. Coarse bits must be removed of course. The

'Arel's Fleur'. Semi-trailer for a place in full sun.

'Berba's Francis Femke'. Attractive trailing fuchsia which tolerates sun.

seed dishes can usually be closed off with their own lids. If not, clingfilm with a rubber band is the solution. Before sowing, the seed compost is firmed and moistened. See to it that the ground does not become a mud bath with water lying on the surface. The seeds are then laid one by one on the surface of the compost, using fine tweezers or a dissecting needle with the point moistened. Fuchsias germinate in light, so the seed can lie on the surface uncovered. With regard to fungus damage in particular, but also in order to prick the seedlings out more easily, place the seeds about 1 cm apart. After sowing, spray the dish with a fungicide which is not too aggressive, and then put the lid on the dish. Normally, the dish remains closed until about a week before pricking out.

As already stated, fuchsias germinate in light. The seed usually germinates quickly at a temperature of 15 - 20° C. It can happen though that

germination does not occur for months. Particularly seed from fuchsias of the *encliandra*-section and hybrids derived from these takes a long time. These plants have relatively large seeds with a thick germination-inhibiting seed coat. So don't be too quick to throw away seeds that have not come up. Once the seed has germinated, the problems start.

It is particularly important that light and heat are in balance. Early on in the year, when there is not yet much daylight, the dishes of seed must be kept in a place which is cool and as light as possible. If young seedlings grow up with too much heat, they become long and straggly, which makes them very vulnerable. Sometimes they can be saved by planting them as deeply as possible with the stalk in the ground up to the seed leaves.

The 'Wilma Versloot'

Fuchsia 'Peredrup'

When the largest seedlings threaten to reach the lid, the dish is opened. If the humidity is low, indoors for example, do not do this all at once. It is better to leave the lid ajar at first. This will harden the seedlings off for pricking out, which is not done until spring. If you have a lot of seedlings, it is pleasant to work with a multi-pot tray, which will take 100 - 150 seedlings in small pre-shaped pots. For smaller numbers it is better to work with 5 cm diameter pots. If using separate pots, it is useful to label every pot, stating the descent of the seedling concerned. Only when the large plants go outside, is there enough room in the greenhouse to pot on into pots of 9 cm diameter for example. In a pot of this size, a young fuchsia plant can still bloom in the summer and the seedlings can already be selected on their flowering in their first year.

Since all strong plants are valuable eventually, I treat my pricked out seedlings just like rooted cuttings. Of course they have to acclimatise from the protected environment of the seed tray to, for instance the greenhouse climate, before they are pricked out. After that they have to make do with ordinary potting compost suitable for fuchsias and the same care that the cuttings get. The seedlings which can't take this are not suitable for this life. While growing, cuttings must be top-

Fuchsia x bacillaris is a variegated foliage encliandra-crossing. Don't take cuttings from 'green shoots'.

ped to get a nicely-shaped plant with many flowers, fuchsia-hybridists will not top their plants. In the first place they will then bloom earlier – that same year – but in addition it will become evident whether or not the newcomer is self-branching. That is of course an important selection criterium.

Grafting

Actually, the grafting of fuchsias has nothing to do with propagation, as is the case with roses or fruit trees, from which cuttings often cannot be taken.

In most cases grafting is used to create another growth form, such as a real trailer onto a stem or a stem on which different varieties bloom. In some cases this means is used to provide a sturdy base for a cultivar which, due to its weak root system, is difficult to cultivate in our climate. The *F. triphylla*, which is well-known for being very difficult, does considerably better on a rootstock.

For the grafting of fuchsias, two methods are the most obvious: amateurs will have the most success with the method in which a piece of bark from the stem is cut from two young plants in

'Bon Accord' has erect flowers and therefore does well as a bedding plant. It is, alas, rather sensitive to botrytis, so ensure that no flowers which have to be topped off remain on the flowers.

such a way that the two wounds which are created fit exactly over each other. To fix them together teflon gas-fitter's tape can be used, which immediately protects the wounds from drying out and possible infections.

When the graft has taken, the top can be cut off just above the fusion with the rootstock and the rooting part of the crown just below this. Just as with most things concerning growth, grafting of fuchsias succeeds best in the spring. It speaks for itself that the greenhouse environment offers the best opportunities for this.

Left: Fuchsia 'Celia Smedley' rootstock for 9 grafts.

Below: "Vobeglo' is a little troublesome, but with a bit of luck it is an ideal annual bedding plant.

CHAPTER 7

Combatting pests and diseases

Wild plants in their natural surroundings are perfectly capable of putting up resistance to harmful organisms occurring there. Plants which cannot, do not survive and so continuous natural selection takes place, in which the fittest survive. Plants which are brought into another environment, with a different climate and other threatening organisms, need help. Certainly when this concerns cultivated plants which, through hybridisation, have also received other properties. If we then put these plants in large collections in our gardens as monoculture we cannot avoid sometimes devastating damage, especially from insects, mites and fungi. The only thing left to us is: (mostly chemical) combat.

'Alison Ryle' is a problem-free upright fuchsia.

Family relationships

The *Fuchsia* is one of the plant genera within the family *Onagraceae*, a large family with representatives all over the world. If you hold an evening primrose flower upside down, you will see that it looks like a yellow fuchsia flower. In western Europe too, relations of the fuchsia can be found in the wild. Apart from the various species of evening primrose, these are the rosebay willow-herb and the representatives of the genus *Epilobium* (fireweed). Most of the representatives of the evening primrose family grow just like the fuchsias in America.

Beautiful ornamental plants from the North American genera such as *Clarkia*, *Gaura*, and *Godetia* have found their way into our gardens. The relations of the fuchsia, beautiful though they are, can form a threat to a fuchsia collection. They serve namely as host plant for a number of organisms which threaten the fuchsias as pests. As far as the caterpillar of the beautiful elephant hawk moth is concerned, this is not great disaster.

Above: 'Tomma', a beautiful acquisition from Lutz Bögemann from Germany, is problem-free.

Right: 'Golden Anniversary'. A splendid American trailer which gets its name from the 50th anniversary of the founding of the American Fuchsia Society in 1980. It loves a cool place.

'Shy Look' tolerates full sun, but looks better in diffused light. It is sensitive to botrytis.

The caterpillars do not appear in very large numbers and can destroy a few shoots at the most before the culprit is discovered. Please don't kill it. Putting it onto a rosebay willow-herb for instance is a much friendlier solution. The caterpillars, funnily enough, are quite happy with lady bedstraw species, which are definitely not related to fuchsias.

A nastier threat is posed by fuchsia rust (*Pucciniastrum epilobolii*), a fungus that not only seriously damages fuchsias, but also other species of evening primrose. There is not much point in fighting rust in fuchsias if there is an untreated rosebay willow-herb somewhere around which is infested. Rust on non-related plants such as roses is fortunately not harmful to fuchsias.

'Mrs Lovell Swisher' must be topped often to obtain a good plant. It is further a problem-free plant.

Insects

Insects are by far the greatest group of living creatures on our planet. Although small, by their numbers they form an impressive power. In addition to the many species which are useful to mankind, for example for pollinating fruit trees and plants or by combatting harmful vermin, there are unfortunately a number of species which, principally in agriculture and horticulture, can cause destruction or transmit infectious diseases. When combatting insect pests which can also strike fuchsias, it is important to kill the bad insects but not the good ones. Modern insecticides are more and more geared to this. In addition more all-round means can be used: for instance, honey-sucking insects can be saved by spraying with pesticides in the evening when the insects are no longer active.

Spraying pesticides on open flowers should also be avoided as far as possible.

Aphids

Fuchsias can be severely troubled by these tiny creatures. Not, in the first place, by the sap they draw from the plant, but rather through the sugary secretion, the honeydew, forming a sticky film with which they cover the plants. Sooty mould feels very much at home on this and covers the leaves with a dark layer, blocking off the breathing pores of the plant.

If the damage is discovered in time, treatment with a solution of soap and methylated spirits is possible. If the damage is more serious, chemicals which are especially effective on aphids can help, as will insects with a tough chitin shield, such as ladybirds which themselves do no harm.

Leafhoppers

The larvae of this greenish, flying insect are the cause of the trouble.

If you notice that the leaves of your fuchsia plants are beginning to look brown from the point, and going along the edges, you can be pretty sure that your plant is suffering a serious attack from leafhoppers. On the underside of the leaves you will find a few small green insects about 2 mm long, which scuttle away sideways if you try to touch them. It is also possible that you will find their sloughed-off skins. They live, alas, on everything which has leaves. This means that the use of chemical insecticides on fuchsias alone has to be repeated time and time again, because there is a huge source of infection.

Luckily these leafhoppers are very sensitive to all insecticides and you can suffice with toxins which contain natural or synthetic pyrethroids and are not harmful to mammals. Do be careful though with pond creatures. It is not without reason that pyrethrum is used in forms of primitive fishing.

Mealy bugs

Mealy bugs come in all colours, shapes and sizes. Adult bugs look rather like flattened beetles with a lozenge-shaped shell on the back of the thorax. The young mealy bugs look like large aphids, which can move much faster.
You usually only notice that your plants are being attacked by mealy bugs when it is too late. The young leaves and the buds at the end of the stalks are then badly deformed. In leaves deformed at the base, there are even holes. There is no longer any question of flowering. The mealy bugs themselves are seldom seen because, when there is danger, they let themselves fall and usually find good cover under the plant. Fighting them is best done as prevention in early summer, using less harmful insecticides on the basis of pyrethrum or organic fatty acids.

Whitefly

These mini butterflies, immigrated from the tropics, are a good 1 mm long and are very troublesome, especially in the greenhouse. During a serious attack they will fly in a cloud around the plants, if disturbed, but you can find them on the underside of the leaves.
The damage looks the same as that from aphids and arises through the very tiny larvae which

suck the sap from the underside of the leaves and excrete honeydew. In greenhouses, biological warfare is possible with the help of the harmless wasp, *Encarsia Formosa*.

During hot summers these useful creatures operate even in the garden, and lay their eggs in the larvae. The pupae colour from almost transparent to black, and after a time no whitefly comes out, but a wasp. These wasps are, unfortunately, less resistant to cold than whitefly and they die in a frost-free greenhouse in the winter.

In my (much warmer) conservatory I have kept the whitefly under control very successfully for years with this method. Combatting this with

'Monsieur Thibaut' is a problem-free fast-growing upright cultivar, introduced by the well-known French grower Lemoine in 1848.

chemicals is possible, using practically any insecticide on sale. Spraying every other week about four times in all is recommended, because the eggs are not destroyed. Changing the brand of insecticide from time to time reduces the risk of resistant strains. Expensive insecticides specifically for whitefly are, unfortunately, not available in small quantities. A reasonable alternative perhaps is lightly diluted washing-up liquid, which sticks the insects and their larvae to the leaves. A day later the soap, along with the dead insects can be sprayed off the leaves with the garden hose.

Vine weevils

The vine weevil has an extensive repertoire of host plants. At night, when they are active, they eat away the edges of the leaves. This typical feeding pattern is a warning of their presence. Catching them prevents worse damage and this can be done by checking the damaged plants with a torch in the late evening. During the day they hide away under the pots. A flowerpot with a bit of hay in it is very attractive to them and can be used as a trap. The weevils, which are almost exclusively female, can, without even being fertilised, lay hundreds of eggs, through which one weevil is capable of infecting a whole lot of plants.

The real trouble-makers come out of the eggs– the white, caterpillar larvae, later growing to more than 1 cm long. These larvae eat away the roots of the plants, and in fuchsias they often eat away the entire root system. Initially the afflicted plants make shoots in the spring but then suddenly collapse. A check on the soil ball usually reveals a number of larvae or sometimes white pupae. If the root system is damaged all round, the only thing you can do is take cuttings and grow a new plant. Combatting the weevils biologically is possible by infecting the soil with parasitic eelworms which kill specifically the larvae of the vine weevil. Unfortunately, these nematodes need a relative amount of warmth and cannot do much in a cold greenhouse, while the fuchsias are at rest. Chemical insecticides are

'Supernova' is an easy garden fuchsia which tolerates sun. The erect flowers make it an interesting bedding plant for use as an annual.

available but these are seldom completely effective. Keeping bantam hens, which keep the garden free from small vermin without doing too much damage is, where possible, a viable alternative.

Leaf-cutter bees and Elephant Hawk moth caterpillars

Both of these species of insect cause leaf damage, which resembles the damage caused by the vine weevil. The leaf-cutter bee saws regularly-shaped oval cells for her larvae.

Sometimes you find these like small cigars in a space in the bottom of a hanging pot. The leaf-cutter bee does not do real harm, it only causes damage, which is frustrating to the enthusiasts who think it is a sign of vine weevil damage, which is, however, clearly more irregular. The same applies for the damage done by the Elephant Hawk moth caterpillar.

This beautiful caterpillar, which, when in threatening pose, has a frontal appearance a bit like the trunk of an elephant, is easily found on the damaged leaves. Do not kill these magnificent caterpillars.

They are, like most of the Hawk moth caterpillars, quite rare and after pupation produce wonderful butterflies which, attracted by the delicious scent, take nectar from your honey-

'Aunt Juliana' is a large-bloomed semi-trailer which does not tolerate heat well.

suckle and other night-flowering plants. By putting the caterpillars on a rosebay willow-herb for example, you will be helping to conserve them.

Mites

Representatives of this group of the arthropods distinguish themselves by having four pairs of legs, while insects have only three pairs. Mites are included among the arachnids (spiderlike). A number of species sucks the sap from plants, but others parasite on animals. Fuchsias in Europe have so far only been troubled by the red-spider mite.

This could change. Fuchsias in California, once one of the most important centres of the interest in fuchsias, are being threatened by the Brazilian fuchsia gall mite. As a result of this plague, mem-

'Jean' is a semi-trailer for full sun.

bership of the American Fuchsia Society has fallen drastically.

Red spider mite

In periods of heat and drought you often see, particularly in small-leaved fuchsias, that the undersides of the leaves are becoming dull and have light-brown spots. In a later stage of the infestation, the ends of the twigs are covered with an extremely fine spider web, and the leaves begin to dry up.

Examination of the damaged leaves with a magnifying glass shows, if it is mite, very tiny spiderlike creatures. You need experience to see them with the naked eye. Red spider mites are, unfortunately, difficult to combat. Frequent spraying with water, particularly on the undersides of the leaves, helps a bit but is not totally effective. Only the use of systemic pesticides is of any real help.

Timely discovery and treatment with pesticides which contain organic fatty acids and are reasonably environmentally-friendly, can limit the red spider mite plague.

The Brazilian fuchsia gall mite

We in Europe can thank our lucky stars that, together with plant material originating from America, we haven't yet introduced this organism, specially oriented towards fuchsias. The North Americans did that in 1981. The gall mite mainly damages the sprouting ends of branches, where bilious-looking, sometimes a bit reddish, deformities appear.

Badly damaged plants are an ugly sight and they eventually die.

The very tiny mites, with two pairs of legs which are reduced, can only be seen under a powerful magnifying glass. They spread very quickly with the wind.

There are hopes that they will not be able to survive in the cool climate of Northern Europe and the northern parts of the United States, but this is not sure. The descendants of *M. Magellanica*, in particular, which form the larger part of our cultivars, are extremely sensitive.

The Americans are considering cultivating a whole new fuchsia stock with other ancestors. For the moment, the best method of combat is not to import fuchsias from America. Should this plague strike in Europe, this could mean the end of the current fuchsia rage. Adequate control is possible with systemic toxins.

Fungi

Fungi can give fuchsia-lovers a whole lot of trouble, if only because their spores are so fine and often so numerous that infection of the plants is inevitable, if the circumstances are favourable. The first precaution is to keep the greenhouse spotlessly clean.

Frequent ventilation and, if that is not possible, keeping the air in motion with the aid of a ventilator can help to make the conditions less favourable for parasitic fungi. It is well known that strong, healthy plants run less risk than weak or young examples.

Botrytis

Grey mould (*botrytis*) attacks dead or rotting material in the first instance. In a warm, moist propagating-tray, it can begin with fallen leaves and subsequently rapidly strike the living young plants.

If you remove this dead material regularly, you will prevent the contents of the tray from becoming completely mouldy. Preventive spraying with fungicide can alleviate the unpleasantness to a large degree. Damage can also occur to mature plants in the greenhouse environment, where it is sometimes damp, and the plants are rarely taken outside. Plants with short internodes and closely positioned leaves are particularly at risk. It is usually enough just to cut away the affected leaves or branches.

Fuchsia rust

Many rust fungi are specific, that is to say, directed towards a certain plant. Thus rust which attacks roses is absolutely harmless to fuchsias. Fuchsia rust does, however. occur on relations to the fuchsia, such as rosebay willow-herb, fire-

'Papy René' is a charming, recent acquisition from France. It is an upright grower for semi-shade.

weed, evening primrose and godetias. The rust is best recognisable by the powdery orange-brown rust patches on the undersides of the leaves. That powder, the spores, are carried by the wind and can infect the whole collection if not discovered in time. It is best to destroy the affected leaves and spray the whole collection, together with any of the above-mentioned related species, with an anti-rust fungicide.

In this context it is wise to prevent infection to new acquisitions by placing them in quarantine for some time. Plants returned after a show should, ideally, be disinfected before they are put back among the other fuchsias.

Blight

Many plants are troubled with blight or mildew, particularly in late summer. Fortunately, this infection is seldom seen on common cultivars, which are descended from *F. magellanica*. Particularly newer products of crossings with other species as ancestor, do, however, appear to be sensitive.

The damage is most easily seen on young leaves and flower stems, which are covered by a whitish film. The risk of infection is greatest during hot and damp weather. Preventive spraying can restrict the extent of the calamity. If the damage is severe, you will have to opt for repeated spraying with fungicides designed for mildew.

Soil fungi

Healthy mature plants have little to fear from these fungi which live in the ground. However, if through over-watering the root system gets into poor condition, they can strike the plant concerned and kill it.

Young plants run more risk and can suddenly die. Without there being anything noticeably wrong, they fall over. Fighting this is not really possible, and the best thing to do is to keep young plants fairly dry.

Combatting pests and diseases in winter

Actually, fuchsias have least to fear from damage during winter. If, however, you have not repotted your plants at the beginning of the winter, damage from vine weevils is, in many cases, a serious problem.

Apart from repotting there is not much you can do about it. Once you notice that plants which have already begun to sprout are dying, only taking fresh cuttings can save the plant for the collection. Keeping a good look-out is the answer. Whitefly and aphids can appear when it begins to get warmer.
The use of a dichlorvos mist spray is almost always sufficient, certainly at an early stage.
Because the greenhouse is an enclosed space, the toxin cannot harm the environment.

Botrytis can best be combatted preventively by keeping the greenhouse spotlessly clean and clearing away all fallen leaves immediately. A vacuum cleaner is a useful tool for getting between the closely-grouped plants.

Young shoots which are affected must be picked off as soon as possible. In propagating trays or other places where young plants are standing close to each other, it is worthwhile spraying with fungicide.

'Quasar' is a trailer with striking blooms for a place in light shade.

List of international associations of fuchsia-lovers

This lists the current correspondence addresses for the various associations. As these are associations for enthusiasts, there are often changes of address. Your own association will usually be able to provide you with a recent address.

Great Britain
British Fuchsia Society
B.C. Morrison, 31 Tennyson Way, Hornchurch, Essex RM12 4BU

Australia
Australian Fuchsia Society
Anne C. Feast, P.O.Box 97, Kent Town, South Australia 5071Western Australian Fuchsia Society
Helen Martin-Beck, 56 Broadbeach blvd., Hillarys, Western Australia 6025

Austria
Oesterreichische Fuchsienfreunde
Elisabeth Schnedl, Wiener Straße 216, 8051 Graz

Belgium
De Vlaamse Fuchsiavrienden vzw
Oscar Defeu, Hoge Akker 25, 2930 Brasschaat
De Vrije Fuchsiavrienden vzw
Erna van Wiele, Lijkveldestraat 100,
9170 Sint-PauwelsLes Amis du Fuchsia
Michel Cornet, Rue du Moulin 24, 6230 Pont-à-Celles

Canada
B.C. Fuchsia & Begonia Society
Lorna Herchenson, 2402 Swinburne Ave.,
North Vancouver, B.C. V7H 1L2

Denmark
Dansk Fuchsia Klub
Henrik Andersen, Arnevangen 56, Søllerød,
DK 2840 Holte

France
Société Franko-Europeénne de Fuchsiaphilie
1 Rue de la Convention,
93120 la Courneuve

Germany
Deutsche Fuchsien Gesellschaft
Hans-Peter Peters, Pankratius Straße 10,
Groß Förste, D-31180 GiesenDeutsche Dahlien,
Fuchsien und Gladiolen Gesellschaft
Elisabeth Göring, Drachenfells Straße 9a, D-53177 Bonn

Italy
Associazione Italiana della Fuchsia
Prof. Pietro Bonati, Via S. Filippo 13, 13051 Biella (VC)

Netherlands
Nederlandse Kring van Fuchsiavrienden
J.C. Makkinje, Gratamastraat 28, 3067 SE Rotterdam
Ledensecretariaat:
c/o Dhr C.F. Langen, Frans Langeveldlaan 9, 1251 XW Laren tel. ++31 35 5386444

Norway
Norsk Fuchsia Selskap
Jack Haugland, Husebysletta 8, N-3400 Lier

South Africa
South African Fuchsia Society
Mrs D. Raw, P.O.Box 1325, Howick, 3290 R.S.A.
Western Cape Fuchsia Society of South Africa
Sally Davidson, 17 Avenue Rd.,
Rondebosch 7700, Cape Town

Sweden
Svenska Fuchsiasällkapet
Agneta Westin, Östermalmsgatan 68, S-11450 Stockholm

Switzerland
Schweizerischer Fuchsienverein
Vreny Schleeweiss, Grübweg 163,
CH-4451 Wintersingen

United States
American Fuchsia Society
Al Sydnor, Country Fair Building, 9th Avenue & Lincoln Way, San Francisco, Ca 94122
Northwest Fuchsia Society
Ollie de Graaf, P.O.Box 33071, Bitter Lake Station, Seattle, WA 98133

Recommended reading

The checklist of species, hybrids and cultivars of the genus Fuchsia, Leo B. Boullemier, 1985 Blandford Press, Poole, Dorset
English standard work with fuchsia descriptions and data about hybridists.

Fuchsias - The complete guide, 1995 Batsford London. Edwin Goulding, owner of a well-known fuchsia nursery and fuchsia hybridist, recorded much of his knowledge in this fuchsia bible.

Fuchsias - A colour guide, 1996 The Crowood Press Ramsbury. George Bartlett gives descriptions of more than 2000 fuchsias, which are accompanied by more than 700 good colour photos.
Fuchsias, Leo B. Boullemier, 1995 Aura Books. A step-by step garden guide to fuchsias.

INDEX